KETO THANKSGIVING AND CHRISTMAS COOKBOOK

THIS BOOK BELONGS TO

_____

_____

_____

TABLE OF CONTENTS

THANKSGIVING

DESSERTS

Flourless Chocolate-Walnut Cookies	5
Vegan Chocolate Truffles	6
Pecan-crusted blueberry crème fraîche semifreddo	7
Keto Pumpkin Cheesecake	10
Avocado Mousse	12
Keto Pumpkin Pie	12
Pomegranate Orange Tart	14
Keto Peanut Butter Squares	15
Pumpkin Spice Chocolate Chip Cookies	17
Pumpkin Blondies	18
Keto Pumpkin Cookies	19
Pumpkin Fudge	20
Keto Pumpkin Cheesecake	21
Keto Pumpkin Pie	22
Apple Blondies	24
Cranberry Blondies Recipe	25
Keto Pecan Pie Bars	27
Healthy Monster Cookie Bars	28
Cranberry Bread	30

Appetizers

Easy Low-Carb & GF Cheese Platter	31
CRUNCHY KETO ROSEMARY CRACKERS	34
Baked Brie and Pecan Prosciutto Savory Fat Bomb	35
CREAMY KETO SPINACH ARTICHOKE DIP	36
CRUNCHY CHIA SEED CRACKERS	37

Jalapeno popper deviled eggs with bacon 38

CHEESY, KETO STUFFED MUSHROOMS WITH BACON 39

BREAD AND BISCUITS

KETO ALMOND BREAD 40

LOW CARB KETO JALAPEÑO CORNBREAD 41

FLUFFY LOW-CARB KETO BISCUITS 42

Keto Cheese & Bacon Rolls 43

CHEESY GARLIC KETO BREADSTICKS 44

CASSEROLES

Low carb green bean casserole 46

Shredded Zucchini Casserole 47

Loaded Creamy Cauliflower Casserole 48

Cheesy Low Carb Yellow Squash Casserole 49

Side Dishes

Keto Cranberry Sauce 50

Creamy cauliflower mash with keto gravy 51

Low-Carb Zucchini Fries with Spicy Avocado Dipping Sauce 53

Creamy Garlic Parmesan Mushroom Chicken 55

Low Carb Cranberry Relish (keto) 56

CRANBERRY SAUCE 57

DELICIOUSLY PERFECT KETO CREAMED SPINACH 58

CREAMY CAULIFLOWER MASHED 'POTATOES' 59

CRISPY KETO BACON WRAPPED ASPARAGUS 60

SHEET PAN BRUSSELS SPROUTS WITH BACON 60

LOW-CARB CAULIFLOWER MAC AND CHEESE 61

Drinks

KETO PUMPKIN SPICE LATTE 62

Keto Nutella Frappuccino 64

Bulletproof Hot Chocolate 65

CHRISTMAS

Desserts

- Keto Chocolate Chip Cookies ... 66
- LOW CARB KETO PUMPKIN CHEESECAKE RECIPE ... 68
- Dark Chocolate Raspberry Cheesecake Brownies ... 70
- Homemade Almond Roca ... 71
- Keto Peanut Butter Balls ... 72
- Keto Cheese Balls ... 74
- Keto Chocolate Cake ... 75
- Keto Pumpkin Cream Cheese Cupcakes ... 77
- Keto Chocolate Cookies ... 80
- Keto Chocolate Crinkle Cookies ... 81
- Keto Christmas Cookies ... 82
- Snowball Cookies ... 84
- German Cinnamon Stars ... 85

MAIN DISHES

- Roast Duck ... 86
- Lemon & Thyme Keto Roasted Chicken ... 87
- Gluten-Free & Keto Swedish Meatballs ... 89

SIDE DISHES AND SAUCES

- Keto Stuffing ... 91
- Keto Roasted Potatoes ... 92
- Cauliflower Mash - Keto Friendly ... 93
- KETO CHEESY ASPARAGUS RECIPE ... 94
- Keto Cranberry Sauce Recipe (Sugar-Free) ... 95

SNACKS AND NIBBLES

- Keto Almond Flour Crackers ... 96
- KETO SALT AND VINEGAR CHIPS ... 97

No-Bake Whole30 Energy Balls 99
Keto Trail Mix 100
Keto Granola Bars 101
Keto Tortilla Chips 102
Keto Cheese Chips 103

BREAD AND LOAFS

Keto Pull-Apart Bread for Christmas 104
Keto Gingerbread Loaf 105
Quick Cream Cheese Keto Pumpkin Bread 107
Cream Cheese Filled Keto Pumpkin Bread 108

Drinks

Paleo & Keto Hot Chocolate With Marshmallows 110
Keto Hot Chocolate 112
KETO MATCHA LATTE 113
Keto Christmas Margarita 114

DESSERTS

Flourless Chocolate-Walnut Cookies

YIELDS: 15

Ingredients

- 3 ounces of confectioner's sugar
- 3/4 cup of Dutch-process cocoa powder
- 1/2 tsp. kosher salt

- 2 big eggs, at room temp
- 1 tsp. pure vanilla extract
- 1 cup chopped toasted walnuts
- 1/2 cup of bittersweet or dark chocolate chips
- Flaky sea salt

Directions

1. Preheat oven to 350 degrees F. Coat two baking sheets with cooking spray and parchment paper.
2. Whisk sugar, cocoa powder, and salt in a medium bowl. Using an electric mixer, beat eggs and vanilla together. Mix in sugar mixture, then fold in walnuts and chocolate chips.
3. Scoop cookie dough (about 1 1/2 tablespoons per cookie) onto prepared baking sheets, leaving a 2-inch space between each cookie, and sprinkle with flaky sea salt.
4. 12 to 14 minutes, they are switching pan positions once until cookies are puffy and the tops begin to crack. Allow cool 5 minutes on baking sheets, then transfer parchment and cookies to wire racks to cool fully.

Vegan Chocolate Truffles

YIELDS:30

TOTAL TIME:1 hour 20 mins

Ingredients

- 20 ounces of finely chopped dark chocolate (72 percent cacao or more)
- 3/4 cup sugar-free coconut milk (well-stirred)
- Toasted coconut flakes for embellishment

Directions

1. Place half of the chocolate in a bowl. Pour coconut milk that is warm to the touch over chocolate. Cover bowl with a towel and set it aside 5 minutes, then whisk the mixture until it is melted and smooth.
2. Refrigerate bowl until chocolate is firm enough to scoop but not brittle, about 30 minutes. Refrigerate tablespoon-sized balls that have been scooped and rolled onto a piece of parchment paper.
3. In the meantime, place the remaining chocolate in a bowl and microwave it in 30-second increments on high, stirring in between, until smooth and melted.
4. Working one at a time, dip each ball in the melted chocolate and tap off excess. If desired before the chocolate has hardened, sprinkle with toasted coconut flakes.

Pecan-crusted blueberry crème fraîche semifreddo

YIELDS: 10 servings

TOTAL TIME: 9 hours 50 mins

Ingredients

Pecan Crumble, for serving

- 1/3 cup pecans whole
- one-third cup of all-purpose flour
- 3 tablespoons of brown sugar
- 1/4 tsp. kosher salt
- 1/8 tsp cinnamon powder

- 3 tbsp. unsalted butter, at room temp

Blueberry Sauce/Filling

- 8.6 c (about 2.5 dry pints) succulent blueberries
- 1/3 c. sugar
- Kosher salt
- Fresh lemon juice, 3-4 teaspoons

Semifreddo Base

- 1 1/4 cups rich cream
- 8 oz. crème Fraiche
- 4 big eggs
- 2/3 c. sugar
- 1 vanilla bean, seeds scraped
- Kosher salt

Directions

Create a pecan crumble by:

1. Preheat oven350 degrees F. Pulse pecans, flour, sugar, salt, and cinnamon in a food processor until pecans are finely minced.
2. Add butter and pulse to incorporate. Spread on parchment-lined baking sheet. If loose, pinch some blueberry-sized clumps; layout and bake, stirring halfway through, for 20 to 22 minutes, until gently browned. Let cool. To yield 1 1/3 cups. Set aside for serving.

To prepare blueberry sauce or filling:

1. Combine blueberries, sugar, 2/3 cup water, and a large pinch of salt in a large saucepan and bring to a boil over heat, stirring occasionally. Reduce heat and simmer, stirring periodically, for 25 to 35 minutes,

until berries have softened and the sauce has thickened (you should have about 3 cups of sauce). Add lemon juice to taste and stir (sauce should be sweet with a slightly tart edge). Refrigerate half of the mixture. Cover and refrigerate while preparing the semifreddo foundation.

Make semifreddo base:

1. Place the mixing bowl of an electric mixer in the refrigerator or freezer to chill. In a medium pot, rapidly simmer 1 1/2 inches of water. Line an 8-cup capacity loaf pan (10 by 5 by 3 inches) with plastic wrap, leaving an overhang on all four edges. In a chilled bowl fitted with the whisk attachment of an electric mixer, combine heavy cream and crème Fraiche at low speed. Increase speed medium and beat for 1 to 1 1/2 minutes, or until medium-soft peaks appear (do not overmix; mixture should be neither stiff nor soupy). Refrigerate the mixture until ready for use.

2. Clean mixing bowl and whisk attachment, then combine the eggs, sugar, vanilla bean seeds, and 1/4 teaspoon of salt in the clean mixing bowl. Place over (but not in) a pan of simmering water and whisk until mixture is extremely hot, beginning to lighten in color, and turning frothy (160°F on an instant-read thermometer), approximately 4 to 5 minutes. Remove mixture from water bath and, using an electric mixer fitted with the whisk attachment, beat on high 6 to 10 minutes, or until mixture is cold, has lightened in color, and has approximately tripled in volume. Fold the cooled crème Fraiche mixture into the egg mixture in two increments until just incorporated.

3. Spread about a third of the semifreddo base equally on the bottom of the prepared pan. Drizzle approximately one-third of the pureed blueberry mixture over the base and use a butter knife to create a marbled effect. Repeat twice more with the remainder of the semifreddo base and sauce. Fold plastic overhangs to cover the top of the semifreddo lightly and freeze for at least 8 hours, or until firm.
4. To serve, remove the semifreddo's top and flip it onto a serving tray or cutting board. Rest until edges soften at room temperature. Slice and serve with the remaining blueberry sauce and Pecan Crumble if preferred.

Keto Pumpkin Cheesecake

YIELDS: 16 SERVINGS
PREP TIME: 0 HOURS 10 MINS
TOTAL TIME: 7 HOURS 30 MINS

INGREDIENTS

FOR THE CRUST

- 1 1/2 cups almond flour
- 1/4 c. coconut flour
- 2 tbsp. granulated Swerve
- 1/2 teaspoon of cinnamon
- 1/4 tsp. kosher salt
- 7 tbsp. butter, melted

FOR THE RECIPE

- 4 (8-ounce) bricks of softened cream cheese

- 1/2 cups of brown sugar
- 1 c. pumpkin purée
- 3 big eggs
- 1 tsp. pure vanilla extract
- 1 gram of cinnamon
- 1/2 tsp. ground ginger
- 1/4 tsp. kosher salt
- whipped cream as an embellishment
- Pecans, chopped and toasted, for garnish

DIRECTIONS

1. Preheat oven to 350 degrees. Combine almond flour, coconut flour, Swerve, cinnamon, and salt in a medium bowl. Add melted butter and blend thoroughly. Press crust in an 8-inch springform pan. For 10 to 15 minutes, bake until gently browned.
2. Reduce oven to 325 degrees. Combine cream cheese and swerve in a large bowl and mix until fluffy. Add pumpkin purée and beat until no lumps remain. Beat each egg until smooth. Add vanilla, cinnamon, ginger, and salt. Pour the batter over the crust, then use an offset spatula to smooth the surface.
3. Wrap the pan's bottom with aluminum foil and place it in a big roasting pan. Pour enough boiling water to fill the baking dish halfway.
4. bake for approximately one hour or until the middle of the cheesecake barely jiggles. Turn off the heat, prop open the oven door, and cool the cheesecake in the oven for one hour.

5. Remove the wrap and refrigerate the cheesecake for at least 5 hours and up to 1 day, or until totally cooled.
6. Serve topped with whipped cream and toasted pecans.

Avocado Mousse

YIELDS: 2 servings
TOTAL TIME: 0 hours 5 mins

Ingredients

- 1 big ripe avocado
- 1/4 cup of Dutch-process cocoa
- 3 tablespoons of unsweetened almond milk
- 2 tablespoon honey
- 1 tsp. pure vanilla extract
- salt

Directions

1. Puree avocado, cocoa, almond milk, honey, vanilla extract, and a bit of salt in a tiny food processor. Refrigerate if desired.
2. Garnish with chocolate shavings.

Keto Pumpkin Pie

YIELDS: 16 SERVINGS
PREP TIME: 0 HOURS 15 MINS
TOTAL TIME: 3 HOURS 30 MINS

INGREDIENTS

FOR THE CRUST

- 1 1/2 cups almond flour
- 3 tbsp. coconut flour
- 1/4 tsp. baking powder
- 1/4 tsp. kosher salt
- 4 tbsp. butter, melted
- 1 large egg, beaten

FOR THE FILLING

- 1 (15-oz.) can of pumpkin puree
- 1 cup rich cream
- 1/2 c. keto-friendly brown sugar, such as Swerve that is packed
- 3 big eggs, beaten
- 1 tsp of cinnamon powder
- 1/2 tsp of ginger powder
- 1/4 tsp of nutmeg powder
- 1/4 teaspoon of clove powder
- 1/4 tsp. kosher salt
- 1 tsp. pure vanilla extract
- Cream whipped for serving (optional)

DIRECTIONS

1. Preheat oven to 350 degrees. Whisk almond flour, coconut flour, baking powder, and salt in a large bowl. Melted butter and egg make a dough. Puncture a 9-inch pie crust with a fork.
2. Bake until lightly golden, 10 minutes.

3. Thoroughly combine pumpkin, cream, brown sugar, eggs, spices, and vanilla in a large bowl. Pour the pumpkin mixture into the crust that has been partially baked.
4. 45 to 50 minutes, or until the center of the filling is slightly jiggly, and the crust is golden brown.
5. Turn oven off and prop door open. Allow pie to cool for one hour in the oven before refrigerating until ready to serve.
6. If preferred, serve with whipped cream.

Pomegranate Orange Tart

YIELDS:8

TOTAL TIME:1 hour 20 mins

Ingredients

- 1 1/2 c. walnuts
- 1/2 cup almond flour
- 2 tablespoons of heated vegan butter or coconut oil
- 5 tablespoons of pure maple syrup, divided
- 4 tbsp of peeled, quartered beets (about 1 medium beet)
- 2 c. pomegranate juice
- 1 1/2 c. oat milk
- 1/4 c. pomegranate molasses
- 1 teaspoon of orange zest
- 1 tablespoon of freshly squeezed orange juice
- 1 tsp. pure vanilla extract
- 2 tsp. agar agar

- 2/3 c. pomegranate seeds

Directions

1. Preheat oven 350 degrees F. Sprays a removable-bottom 9-inch tart pan with nonstick cooking spray. Line with parchment paper; spray with cooking spray.
2. Pulse walnuts and almond flour in a food processor to make fine crumbs. Add vegan butter and 2 tablespoons of maple syrup, then pulse to create a sticky dough. Transfer dough to the pan and uniformly press the bottom and sides. Puncture with a fork, then freeze for 5 minutes. Bake 9 to 11 minutes until golden.
3. In the meantime, bring the beets and pomegranate juice to a simmer in a small saucepan and cook until soft, 30 to 45 minutes.
4. Transfer the beets and liquid (there should be around a quarter cup of juice) to a blender. Puree the oat milk, molasses, orange zest and juice, vanilla, and remaining 3 tablespoons of maple syrup until smooth. Add agar and blend for thirty seconds.
5. Boil the beet mixture. Reduce the heat and simmer 2 minutes. Cool for 5 minutes before straining into the tart shell. Allow it to stand at room temperature until firm and cold, approximately 1 hour. To serve, remove the tart from the pan and sprinkle the edges with pomegranate seeds.

Keto Peanut Butter Squares

YIELDS:12

PREP TIME: 0 HOURS 5 MINS

TOTAL TIME: 2 HOURS 15 MINS

INGREDIENTS

- cooking spray for skillet
- 1 1/2 tablespoons of smooth, unsweetened peanut butter
- 1 1/4 c. coconut flour
- 1/4 cup of keto-friendly powdered sugar, like Swerve
- 1 tsp. pure vanilla extract
- Pinch kosher salt
- 2 cups of keto-compatible chocolate chips
- 2 tbsp. coconut oil
- One tablespoon of flaky sea salt for garnish

DIRECTIONS

1. Prepare an 8" × 8" baking dish with parchment paper and cooking spray. Combine peanut butter, coconut flour, powdered sugar, vanilla, and salt in a medium bowl. Pour into pan and spread evenly with a spatula. Place in the freezer for thirty minutes to harden.
2. Medium microwave-safe bowl, chocolate chips, coconut oil. Stir every 30 seconds in the microwave until the mixture is smooth and pourable. Pour and smooth the chocolate over the peanut butter layer.
3. Garnish with flaky sea salt and place in the freezer for two hours or overnight to firm.
4. Remove peanut butter bars from the baking dish and cut them into squares when ready to serve.

Pumpkin Spice Chocolate Chip Cookies

Prep Time: 5 minutes

Cook Time: 12 minutes

Total Time: 17 minutes

Servings: 12 Cookies

Ingredients

- 1 1/4 cups gluten-free all-purpose flour, if necessary
- 1/2 teaspoon baking powder
- 1/2 teaspoon baking soda
- 1 teaspoon pumpkin pie seasoning
- 1/4 teaspoon salt
- 2/3 cup sugar
- 1/3 cup coconut oil softened
- 1/4 cup desired milk. I utilized almond milk that was not sweetened.
- 1 teaspoon vanilla extract
- 1 cup of your preferred chocolate chips

Instructions

1. Preheat oven to 180°C/350°F. Prepare a big baking sheet or tray with parchment paper and set it aside.
2. In a large dish, combine the dry ingredients and set them aside. Whisk together your sugar and oil in a separate bowl until shiny. Mix the milk and vanilla extract until thoroughly blended. Fold your dry ingredients gently and thoroughly. Using a rubber spatula, incorporate chocolate chunks into the batter.

3. Using a cookie scoop or big spoon, scoop out 12 cookie dough balls and lay them on the prepared baking sheet. Sprinkle the cookies with additional pumpkin pie spice and bake for 12 to 15 minutes, or until the edges turn brown.
4. Cool on the baking sheet.

Notes

- Pumpkin biscuits can be stored at ambient temperature, in an airtight container, or under complete protection. The cookies have a five-day shelf life. Refrigerate them if you wish for them to last longer.
- Wrap each cookie in parchment paper and freeze in a bag or shallow container. Maximum six-month freezer storage. Once ready for consumption, defrost to room temperature.

Pumpkin Blondies

Prep Time: 5 minutes

Cook Time: 30 minutes

Total Time: 35 minutes

Servings: 12 blondies

Ingredients

- 2/3 cup pumpkin puree
- 2/3 cup peanut butter
- 2/3 cup coconut sugar
- 1/4 cup coconut oil softened
- 1 big egg
- 1/2 teaspoon vanilla extract
- 1 cup almond flour
- 1/4 cup coconut flour

- 1 teaspoon baking soda
- 1 tablespoon pumpkin pie seasoning
- 1/4 teaspoon salt
- 1 cup of chocolate chips

Instructions

1. Preheat the oven to 180 degrees Celsius/350 °F. Prepare a pan measuring 8 × 8 inches with parchment paper and set aside.
2. In the bowl of an electric mixer or a large mixing basin, combine the pumpkin, peanut butter, egg, coconut sugar, coconut oil, and vanilla. Add the dry ingredients with care until just mixed. I am combining the chocolate chips.
3. Transfer the batter to the prepared pan and spread it out evenly. Extra chocolate chips and pumpkin pie spice are sprinkled on top. Bake your blondies for 30 to 35 minutes, or until a skewer inserted into the center comes out clean.
4. Remove the blondies from the oven and let them cool completely in the pan before cutting them into bars.
5. Any smooth nut or seed butter will suffice.
6. Use either brown sugar or a brown sugar alternative.
7. If you want to consume these blondies within two days, you may store them at room temperature. Ensure that the blondies are sealed or completely covered. Refrigerate them for up to two weeks to preserve them.
8. Wrap the blondies in parchment paper and place them in a ziplock bag or shallow container to freeze them. Keep for 6 months.

Keto Pumpkin Cookies

Prep Time: 5 minutes

Cook Time: 5 minutes

Total Time: 10 minutes

Servings: 20 Cookies

Ingredients

- 2 cups of nut or seed butter may be substituted for the peanut butter.
- 1/2 cup keto maple syrup
- 3/4 cup coconut flour
- 2 teaspoons pureed pumpkin
- 1 teaspoon pumpkin pie spice

Instructions

1. In a microwave-safe bowl or on the stovetop, warm the peanut butter and maple syrup. Whisk until thoroughly blended.
2. Add the remaining ingredients and thoroughly combine until a thick, solid batter remains. If the batter is too watery, add additional coconut flour.
3. Form little dough balls with your hands and set them on a lined dish. Press each ball into the shape of a cookie and crisscross them with a fork. Refrigerate until hard.
4. *Additional coconut flour may be required if the batter is too thin.
5. STORAGE: Pumpkin cookies without baking should be refrigerated, and covered, for up to four weeks.
6. Wrap each cookie in parchment and store in a bag or container. Freeze for up to six months.

Pumpkin Fudge

Prep Time: 5 minutes

Cook Time: 30 minutes

Total Time: 35 minutes

Servings: 12 pieces

Ingredients

- 2 cups of cashew butter
- 5 tbsp keto maple syrup
- 1/2 cup pumpkin puree
- 1/2 cup coconut oil
- 1 tbsp optional Pumpkin pie spice

Instructions

1. Line an 8-by-8-inch baking dish with aluminum foil or parchment paper and set aside.
2. In a microwave-safe bowl or on the stovetop, combine cashew butter and coconut oil and melt. Stir the pure maple syrup into the pumpkin puree until thoroughly blended. Optional pumpkin pie spice topping.
3. Chill the mixture in a parchment-lined baking dish.

Notes

- Pumpkin Fudge must be refrigerated in the refrigerator, in an airtight container, or plastic wrap.
- Additionally, fudge is freezer-safe and keeps nicely in the freezer. It is perishable for up to six months.

Keto Pumpkin Cheesecake

Prep Time: 15 minutes
Cook Time: 5 minutes
Total Time: 20 minutes
Servings: 12 servings

Ingredients

- 1 keto graham cracker crust recipe

- 1 cup rich cream
- 16 ounces dairy-free cream cheese, if necessary
- 15 ounces of unsweetened pumpkin puree
- 1 cup sugar-free confectioners' sugar
- 1 teaspoon vanilla extract
- 1 teaspoon cinnamon
- 1/2 teaspoon nutmeg
- 1/4 teaspoon salt

Instructions

1. Prepare and refrigerate your graham cracker crust while preparing the filling.
2. Whip heavy cream until firm peaks form. Cream cheese should be beaten in a separate bowl until light and fluffy. Add pumpkin puree and beat until there are no lumps. Add powdered sugar and beat until there are no more lumps. Add vanilla, cinnamon, nutmeg, and salt, and combine with a mixer. Fold in the whipped cream until barely incorporated.
3. Transfer the filling into the prepared pie shell. To firm, refrigerate overnight.
4. This recipe fits an 8-inch springform pan.

TO STORE: Refrigerate the cheesecake while loosely wrapped. It will remain fresh for one week.

To freeze: The pumpkin cheesecake can be frozen as a whole cheesecake or as individual slices. Use a big, freezer-safe container to enclose the food properly. Safely freeze for six months.

Keto Pumpkin Pie

Prep Time: 10 minutes

Cook Time: 35 minutes

Total Time: 45 minutes

Servings: 8 servings

Ingredients

For the crust

- 3/4 cup coconut flour
- 1/4 teaspoon salt
- 2 teaspoon sugar-free confectioners' sugar
- 2 big eggs
- 1/3 cup coconut oil melted

For the filling of pumpkin pie

- 15 ounces unsweetened pumpkin puree
- 1 1/4 cups desired milk. I utilized almond milk that was not sweetened.
- 3/4 cup keto maple syrup
- 1 teaspoon of cinnamon
- 1 tablespoon powdered arrowroot

Instructions

For the tart pastry

1. Grease a pie dish of nine inches with oil and set it aside.
2. All components should be blended or processed until crumbly.
3. Form a ball of dough and knead it till smooth using your hands. Using a rolling pin, roll out the dough to a thickness of around half an inch. Push the dough into an oiled pie dish. Press it carefully into the pie pan if the dough begins to crumble. Decorate the sides of the dish with a fork. Refrigerate.

For the filling of pumpkin pie

1. In a saucepan, combine the pumpkin puree, milk, syrup, cinnamon, and arrowroot powder by stirring thoroughly. Stir until the sauce thickens and boils.
2. Put the hot filling in a big basin. Allow for 2 minutes before blending well with a stick blender until smooth and creamy. Cool for five minutes.

Putting together and baking the pie

1. Preheat the oven to 180 degrees Celsius/350 °F.
2. Transfer the filling for the pumpkin pie into the pie crust. Bake the pumpkin pie's crust for 35 to 40 minutes, or until golden brown.
3. Cool the pie at room temperature. Once the filling has cooled, refrigerate it to firm up.

Notes

- Pumpkin pie should always be refrigerated, completely covered, and stored in the refrigerator. It lasts two weeks.
- You can freeze the pie either as a whole pie or as separate slices. Keep it in a suitable container for freezing and store it in the freezer for up to six months. Defrost at ambient temperature or overnight in the refrigerator.

Apple Blondies

Prep Time: 5 minutes

Cook Time: 25 minutes

Total Time: 30 minutes

Servings: 9 Blondies

Ingredients

- 1/2 cup apple sauce unsweetened

- Any nut or seed butter can be substituted for 1/2 cup almond butter
- 1/4 cup coconut flour
- Three to four tablespoons of keto maple syrup may be substituted for pure maple syrup or agave if not entirely keto.
- 1 tablespoon apple pie spice
- 1/4 cup Preferred Granulated Sweetener Optional

Instructions

1. Preheat oven 180C/350F and line an 8-by-8-inch baking dish with parchment paper.
2. In a large mixing basin, thoroughly incorporate all ingredients until a fairly thick batter is created.
3. Sprinkle granulated sweetener on prepared baking dish. 30 minutes in the oven, or until the tops are golden brown.
4. Bring to room temperature. Before slicing, chill for at least one hour in the refrigerator.

Notes

- Depending on the kind of coconut flour used, you may need to add tablespoon of coconut flour OR maple syrup to achieve a "firm" batter.
- Healthy Apple Pie Blondies should be stored in the refrigerator. They are perishable for up to two weeks.
- Apple pie blondies made without flour are freezer-friendly and can be frozen for six months.

Cranberry Blondies Recipe

Prep Time: 10 minutes

Cook Time: 20 minutes

Servings: 12 Blondies

Ingredients

- 1 tbsp flaxseed meal Can substitute for one big egg
- 1 cup almond flour, blanched
- 2 tbsp coconut flour
- 2 teaspoons of your preferred granulated sweetener
- One-half cup almond butter
- 1/4 cup of desired milk
- 1/2 teaspoon vanilla extract
- 14 cup unsweetened dried cranberries
- 1/4 cup choice of chocolate chips

Instructions

1. Preheat the oven to 180 degrees Celsius/350 °F. Prepare a pan measuring 8 × 8 inches with parchment paper and set aside.
2. Flax egg: Combine ground flaxseed and 3 tablespoons water. Allow sitting for ten minutes or until a gel forms.
3. In a large mixing basin, thoroughly combine the dry ingredients. In a bowl, thoroughly combine the almond butter, flax egg (or egg), milk, and vanilla essence.
4. Incorporate the wet mixture into the dry mixture thoroughly. Fold in the cranberries and chocolate chips, reserving a few to sprinkle on top of the blondies.
5. Spread blondie batter in the prepared pan. Bake 20 to 25 minutes, or until golden brown and a toothpick comes out 'just' clean.
6. Cool the blondies in the pan before cutting them into bars.

Notes

For extremely gooey cranberry chocolate chip bars, remove them at around 20 minutes from the oven.

Cranberry blondies stored at room temperature for five days. Blondies can be preserved in the refrigerator for up to seven days. These blondies are suitable for freezing and will store well for six months.

Keto Pecan Pie Bars

Prep Time: 10 minutes
Cook Time: 40 minutes
Servings: 12 Bars

Ingredients

For the shortbread crust

- 1 cup coconut flour
- 3 tbsp keto maple syrup
- 1/3 cup coconut oil can substitute for butter

As the gooey pecan topping,

- 1/2 cup coconut oil
- 5 tbsp keto maple syrup
- 2/3 cup of your preferred granulated sweetener
- 1/4 teaspoon salt
- 2 cups pecans

Instructions

1. Preheat the oven to 180 degrees Celsius/350 °F. Prepare a pan measuring 8 × 8 inches with parchment paper and set aside.
2. In a mixing bowl, thoroughly incorporate the coconut flour, syrup, and coconut oil (or butter) until crumbly but firm. Push into the baking dish. Bake for 10-12 minutes, until brown.

3. During the baking of the shortbread, prepare the pecan topping.
4. In a small saucepan, cook the syrup, coconut oil, granulated sugar, and salt over medium heat. Once the granulated sweetener has melted, and the mixture has begun to bubble, add the pecans and continue cooking for 1 minute before removing the pan from the heat.
5. Remove the shortbread from the oven, then spread the pecan caramel mixture over the entire surface of the shortbread. Bake for 5 minutes or until topping bubbles. Do not overbake, or the topping will become dry.
6. Allow the pecan pie bars to cool completely after removing them from the oven. Once cooled, refrigerate for one hour to solidify. Cut into bars.
7. Pecan Pie Bars should be refrigerated in the refrigerator, in an airtight container, or plastic wrap. They can be stored for two weeks.
8. The bars are suitable for freezing and can be kept frozen for six months.

Healthy Monster Cookie Bars

Prep Time: 5 minutes

Cook Time: 20 minutes

Servings: 12 Bars

Ingredients

- 1 tbsp flaxseed meal
- 1 cup almond flour, blanched
- 2 tbsp coconut flour
- 1 cup of your preferred granulated sweetener
- 1/2 cup nut or seed butter can replace almond butter.
- 1/4 cup coconut milk

- 1/2 teaspoon vanilla extract
- 14 to 12 cup healthy M&Ms; see post for alternatives
- 1/4 cup choice of chocolate chips Optional

Instructions

1. Combine your ground flaxseed with three tablespoons of water to make a flax egg. Allow sitting for ten minutes or until a gel forms.
2. Preheat oven to 350F/180C. Prepare a pan measuring 8 × 8 inches with parchment paper and set aside.
3. In a large mixing basin, thoroughly combine the dry ingredients. Thoroughly blend the flax egg, almond butter, coconut milk, and vanilla extract in a small bowl.
4. Mix wet and dry ingredients well. Fold in the chocolate buttons/chips, reserving a few to sprinkle on top of the cookie bars.
5. Pour the cookie bar batter into the prepared pan and evenly distribute. Bake for 20 to 25 minutes, or until the sides are golden and a toothpick inserted into the center comes out 'just' clean.
6. Cool the cookie bars in the pan before slicing.

Notes

- Remove monster cookie bars from the oven at about the 20-minute mark for ultra-gooey bars.
- The Keto Monster Cookie Bars can be stored at room temperature for five days if they are covered and refrigerated.
- Monster cookie bars last seven days in the fridge.
- Healthy Monster cookie bars are freezer-friendly and keep for up to six months when frozen.

Cranberry Bread

Prep Time: 5 minutes

Cook Time: 45 minutes

Total Time: 50 minutes

Servings: 12 Slices

Ingredients

- 2 cups blanched almond flour almond flour
- 2 tablespoons of your preferred granulated sweetener
- 1 teaspoon cinnamon
- 1/4 teaspoon salt
- 1 teaspoon baking powder
- 2 big bananas mashed
- 2 flax eggs Can be used in place of 2 whole eggs
- 1/2 cup coconut oil melted
- 1 teaspoon vanilla extract
- 1/4 cup dried, unsweetened cranberries
- 1/4 cup of your preferred chocolate chips

Instructions

1. Preheat the oven to 180 degrees Celsius (350 degrees F) and line a loaf pan with parchment paper.
2. Combine 2 teaspoons of ground flaxseed with 5 tablespoons of water to make flax eggs. Allow sitting for 10 minutes to gel.
3. In a large mixing basin, thoroughly combine the dry ingredients. Melt the coconut oil in a separate basin. Whisk together your mashed bananas and flax eggs/eggs.

4. Mix wet and dry components. Reserve a few chocolate chips and dried cranberries to sprinkle on top. Pour into the oiled baking dish.
5. Bake for 40-50 minutes (square pans typically take 40 minutes, loaf pans 45-50 minutes), or until a toothpick inserted in the center is clean.
6. Allow cooling completely in the pan before removing and slicing into 12 pieces.

Notes

To save: Cranberry bread should always be refrigerated and stored in an airtight container. Extremely wet, it will perish at room temperature. Bread will remain fresh for up to seven days.

Wrap slices or the entire loaf in parchment paper and place in a ziplock bag or shallow container for freezing. The shelf life of frozen bread is up to six months.

To reheat bread from the refrigerator, heat it for 30 seconds in the microwave or 3 to 4 minutes in a toaster oven. Allow frozen bread to defrost overnight at room temperature or in the refrigerator.

Appetizers

Easy Low-Carb & GF Cheese Platter

Prep Time 20 minutes

Total Time 20 minutes

Servings 12

Ingredients

- 5-ounce Mozzarella balls, often called bocconcini

- 5 ounces Pistachios
- 4 ounces of piquant or marinated stuffed peppers
- 6 ounces Mixed olives
- 4 ounces roasted turkey sliced thinly
- 4 oz Proscuitto rolled into balls
- 4 oz Salami
- 5 ounces Cheddar cheese
- 7 oz Brie
- 7 ounces of flaxseed crackers or build your keto crackers
- 4 oz Almonds
- 1/2 cup Blueberries
- 1 cup of Strawberries

Instructions

1. Choose a cutting board that is not too large so that the ingredients occupy most of the space. This makes the platter appear abundant and brimming.
2. Place three tiny bowls in the approximate center of the board and one bowl in each corner.
3. Add mozzarella balls (bocconcini), pistachios, stuffed peppers (or alternative antipasto), and mixed olives to the bowls.
4. Roll the turkey slices and stack the prosciutto on opposing sides of the board. Layer the salami up on the opposite end to evenly distribute the meats around the board.
5. Next, slice the cheddar cheese and stack it alongside the salami. Add the brie to the opposite end of the dish.

6. The other ingredients, including almonds, blueberries, crackers, and strawberries, should be arranged in the remaining spaces on the board. Additionally, some flax crackers may be placed in a separate bowl. Distribute the little foods, such as nuts and blueberries, in a slightly disorganized manner instead of forming precise small groups. Some overlap of ingredients here is ok.

Notes

- Each serving contains five flaxseed crackers.
- Make-ahead? Make your antipasto dish a few hours ahead and loosely cover with plastic wrap until ready to serve. Store cheeses in the refrigerator until serving time if the weather is warm.
- Taking to a party? For easy transport, build the cheese board on a dish with a raised rim and cover it with cling film, or assemble it when you arrive at the party.
- How can I make the dish appear delectable? Abundance is the key to making an antipasto dish appear gorgeous. The board should be brimming with an assortment of colorful and tasty dishes. The first step is to have ample food; you don't want the board or dish to be too visible (and a board that is not too large).
- Arrange everything for contrast so that, for instance, the cheeses are dispersed over the platter and not all in one location.
- Use small containers for fruit and nuts to create distinct zones if desired.
- Pro styling tip! Introduce some disorder by dropping a few nuts or berries throughout the board. Your platter should be a visual as well as a gustatory delight.

CRUNCHY KETO ROSEMARY CRACKERS

Total Time: 35 minutes

Yield: 15 crackers 1x

INGREDIENTS

- 1 large complete egg
- 1 tablespoon olive oil
- 3 to 4 teaspoons of water
- 1/2 teaspoon salt
- 1/4 teaspoon pepper
- 2 teaspoons of rosemary
- 1/2 teaspoon of garlic powder
- 1/2 cup almonds
- 1/2 cup pecans
- 1 cup pumpkin seeds
- 1/4 cup flax meal

INSTRUCTIONS

1. Prepare a large parchment-lined baking sheet and preheat the oven to 325 degrees. Set aside
2. Beat egg with water, olive oil, salt, pepper, garlic powder, and finely chopped rosemary in a small bowl.
3. Add nuts and seeds to a large food processor bowl and pulse on high until roughly chopped. Stir in flax meal to mix. Pour in liquid mixture and pulse just until mixed
4. Roll out the mixture on parchment paper to a thickness of 1/6 inch. Cut into uniform pieces and place on a baking pan.

5. Bake for thirty minutes, or until golden and crisp.

Baked Brie and Pecan Prosciutto Savory Fat Bomb

Serves: 1 serving

Serving size: 1 serving

Ingredients

- 1 slice prosciutto, about ½ ounce
- 1 ounce of full-fat Brie cheese
- 6 pecan halves, approximately 1/3 oz
- 1/8 teaspoon ground pepper

Instructions

1. Preheat oven to 350 degrees Fahrenheit. Utilize a muffin tray with approximately 2.5" broad and 1.5" deep holes.
2. Fold the piece of prosciutto in half so that it becomes nearly square.
3. Place it in each muffin tin hole to completely line it.
4. Cut the Brie into small cubes, leaving the white rind intact. Place the Brie in the cup lined with prosciutto.
5. Place the pecan halves in between the Brie.
6. Bake 12 minutes, or until the Brie is melted and the prosciutto is cooked.
7. Wait 10 minutes before removing.

CREAMY KETO SPINACH ARTICHOKE DIP

Cook Time: 25 minutes

Total Time: 35 minutes

Yield: 2 cups 1x

INGREDIENTS

- 1/2 cup grated parmesan
- 1/2 cup mozzarella cheese (shredded)
- 1/4 cup dietary yeast
- 10 ounces frozen spinach (thawed and drained)
- 12 ounces of artichoke hearts
- two bulbs of garlic (finely chopped)
- 1/4 cup sour cream
- 1/2 cup of cream cheese
- 1/4 cup mayonnaise
- 1/2 tsp salt
- 1/4 tsp pepper
- 1 teaspoon of garlic powder

INSTRUCTIONS

1. Preheat oven to 375 degrees Celsius.
2. Mix everything in a basin. Mix until all ingredients are thoroughly blended. Pour into a glass pie plate or shallow baking dish. Adding additional cheese is optional.
3. 3. Bake for 20-25 minutes.

CRUNCHY CHIA SEED CRACKERS

Prep Time: 5 minutes

Cook Time: 15 minutes

Total Time: 35 minutes

Yield: 35 crackers 1x

INGREDIENTS

- ½ cup almond flour
- ½ cup chia seeds
- ⅛ tsp salt
- 1 big egg, beaten
- Coarse salt
- pepper freshly cracked

INSTRUCTIONS

1. Preheat oven to 325 degrees Celsius.
2. Add almond flour, chia seeds, and salt to a mixing bowl. Whisk until completely incorporated.
3. Add the beaten egg to the bowl of dry ingredients and knead the mixture with your hands.
4. Spray two parchment paper sheets with cooking spray. Place one piece, sprayed side up, in the center of the dough. Place the second piece, spray-side down, on the dough and lightly press.
5. Roll out the dough into an extremely thin sheet using a rolling pin.
6. Remove and discard the top parchment paper sheet. Carefully put a baking sheet beneath the dough-covered parchment paper.
7. Cut the dough into crackers of the desired size using a pizza cutter or knife.
8. On top of the dough, sprinkle coarse salt and black pepper.
9. Bake the crackers for fifteen minutes.

10. Remove the crackers from the oven and let them cool for fifteen minutes before breaking them apart.

Jalapeno popper deviled eggs with bacon

INGREDIENTS

- 6 big eggs
- 16 sliced pickled jalapenos, split
- Six pieces of bacon, crisply fried and crumbled
- 4 to 6 tablespoons mayonnaise
- 2 ounces of softened cream cheese
- ¼ teaspoon smoked paprika

INSTRUCTIONS

1. The eggs are hard-boiled. This is how I cook eggs to perfection. In a large saucepan, combine eggs and cold water. Add enough water to submerge the eggs completely. Bring water to a vigorous boil over high heat. Once the water has reached a boil, remove the pan from the heat, cover, and let the contents settle for 12 minutes.
2. Chop four jalapeño pieces and keep them aside.
3. The eggs are peeled and cut in half lengthwise. Remove yolks and mash them with a fork in a medium bowl. Add bacon, mayonnaise, cream cheese, and diced jalapenos to the bowl. Mix until all ingredients are thoroughly blended.

4. Transfer the mixture to a plastic bag or pastry bag with a spoon. Squeeze the mixture into one corner of the bag and cut that piece off. Use this to fill the egg halves with the filling.
5. Top each egg with a slice of jalapeño. The paprika is sprinkled over the eggs.

CHEESY, KETO STUFFED MUSHROOMS WITH BACON

Prep Time: 5 minutes
Cook Time: 20 minutes
Total Time: 25 minutes
Yield: 14 stuffed mushrooms 1x

INGREDIENTS

- four thick bacon slices
- 3 ounces of spinach (frozen, thawed, and drained)
- 3 cloves of garlic (finely chopped)
- Four ounces of cream cheese
- 1 big complete egg
- 2 teaspoons coconut flour
- 1 cup mozzarella cheese
- 3/4 teaspoons salt
- 1/4 teaspoon of black pepper
- 16 ounces of baby Bella mushrooms (stems removed, washed, and dried well)

INSTRUCTIONS

1. Preheat oven to 350 degrees F.

2. ignite a big skillet over medium heat on the stovetop. Add bacon to the pan and heat until crispy and browned. Break up the bacon in the pan. Reserve the bacon grease and set the bacon aside.
3. Combine bacon fat, spinach, garlic, cream cheese, egg, coconut flour, mozzarella, salt, and pepper in a large bowl. Add three-quarters of the crumbled bacon and reserve the remainder for the topping.
4. Place the stuffed mushrooms in a shallow baking dish. Spread the remaining bacon crumbles on top.
5. Bake till brown and bubbling, 18-20 minutes. Serve hot.

BREAD AND BISCUITS

KETO ALMOND BREAD

Prep Time: 10 minutes
Total Time: 55 minutes
Yield: 12 slices 1x

INGREDIENTS
- 1/2 cup of butter
- 2 Tbsp coconut oil
- 7 eggs
- 2 cups almond flour

INSTRUCTIONS
1. Preheat the oven to 355 degrees F.
2. Line the inside of a loaf pan with parchment paper.
3. In a bowl, whisk the eggs on high for two minutes.

4. Combine the almond flour, coconut oil, and butter with the eggs. Continue to combine.
5. Transfer the mixture to a loaf pan.
6. Bake for 45 to 50 minutes, or until a toothpick inserted into the center of the cake comes out clean.

LOW CARB KETO JALAPEÑO CORNBREAD

Yield: 12

PREP TIME: 5 MIN

COOK TIME: 25 MIN

TOTAL TIME: 30 MIN

INGREDIENTS

- 2 1/2 tablespoons Red Mill Super-Fine Almond Flour
- 2 1/2 cups shredded cheddar cheese
- 2 jalapenos, seeds removed and chopped finely
- two tablespoons of baking powder
- 1/2 tsp salt
- 3 eggs
- 1/2 cup sour cream
- 1/4 cup grass-fed butter, melted.

INSTRUCTIONS

1. Preheat oven to 350 degrees F and butter a 9 x 13 baking dish.
2. In a large bowl, mix all of the ingredients.
3. Pour batter evenly into baking dish.
4. Bake for 25 minutes, or until the edges are browned slightly.
5. Allow cooling before slicing into 12 even pieces.

FLUFFY LOW-CARB KETO BISCUITS

Prep Time: 10 minutes

Cook Time: 15 minutes

Total Time: 25 minutes

Yield: 12 biscuits 1x

INGREDIENTS

- 1.5 cups almond meal
- 2 teaspoons of cream of tartar
- 1 tsp baking soda
- 1/2 tsp salt
- 1 cup shredded mozzarella
- 4 tbsp butter, softened
- 2 eggs
- 1/4 cup thick heavy cream

INSTRUCTIONS

1. Preheat oven to 400 °F.
2. Combine almond flour, cream of tartar, baking soda, and salt in a mixing dish.
3. In a separate mixing dish, thoroughly incorporate mozzarella, butter, eggs, and heavy whipping cream with a hand mixer.
4. Add dry ingredients to the bowl of wet components and continue mixing with a hand mixer until all ingredients are thoroughly incorporated.
5. Spray a muffin tin and a spoon with cooking spray to prevent sticking.
6. Scoop dough into individual muffin tin molds using a greased spoon.

7. Bake until biscuits are golden.
8. Serve hot and savor!

Keto Cheese & Bacon Rolls

Prep Time: 10 mins
Cook Time: 20 mins
Total Time: 30 mins
Servings: 12 rolls

Ingredients

- 5 ounces Bacon chopped
- 2 teaspoons Cream Cheese
- 2 teaspoons Sesame Seeds
- 1 tablespoon Psyllium Husk
- One-half teaspoon of Baking Powder
- 1 cup Cheddar Cheese shredded
- 1/2 cup Mozzarella Cheese shredded
- 3 big Eggs
- 1/2 teaspoon Pepper powder
- 1 pinch Salt

Instructions

1. Preheating the oven to 180C/355F.
2. Cook diced bacon in a skillet over medium heat until it begins to brown. Turn the heat off.
3. Add the cream cheese to the bacon and let it soften for five minutes while the bacon cools.

4. Place the bacon and cream cheese mixture and the remaining ingredients in a food processor. Reserve a small amount of bacon for topping the rolls.
5. Blend items on medium speed for 3 to 5 minutes.
6. Spoon the mixture into 12 even mounds on baking trays that have been lined. Sprinkle the bacon that was set aside on each roll.
7. Bake for 13 to 16 minutes, or until golden brown and puffy.
8. Warm or refrigerate. They may be reheated quickly in the microwave or toaster oven.

CHEESY GARLIC KETO BREADSTICKS

Prep Time: 20 minutes
Cook Time: 10 minutes
Total Time: 30 minutes
Yield: 5 1x

INGREDIENTS

- 1 cup almond meal
- 1 tablespoon coconut flour
- 1/2 tablespoon baking powder
- 1/2 teaspoon salt
- 1 1/2 tablespoons of garlic powder
- two cups of grated mozzarella
- 2 big eggs
- 1/4 cup of coconut oil or grass-fed butter melted
- 1 teaspoon Italian herb mixture

- 1/4 cup of Asiago or Parmesan cheese, shredded
- 1 tablespoon olive oil

INSTRUCTIONS

1. Preheat the oven to 400 °F.
2. Combine the flour, baking powder, 1 tsp of garlic powder, and salt in a large bowl.
3. Melt mozzarella in microwave-safe bowl. 60-90 seconds on high.
4. Whisk the eggs and coconut oil into the flour mixture, then fold the melted mozzarella into the batter.
5. Work fast while the material is still hot.
6. Flatten the dough on a 9-inch skillet made of cast iron or nonstick.
7. Top with herb mixture, Asiago, and olive oil. Bake for until the cheese on top is golden brown.
8. Remove the dish from the oven and allow it to cool for ten minutes. The flatbread is then transferred to a cutting board and sliced into 10 sticks.

CASSEROLES

Low carb green bean casserole

Yield: Makes 8 Servings 1x

INGREDIENTS

- 1 pound of freshly washed, trimmed, and halved green beans
- 1/2 cup blanched almond meal
- ¼ cup coconut flour

- 1 teaspoon sea salt
- 1/2 teaspoon of black pepper
- 1 small onion, cut thinly
- 2 shallots, cut thinly
- 8 ounces of minced cremini mushrooms
- 2 tablespoons butter
- 3 minced garlic cloves
- 1/2 cup of chicken broth
- 1/2 cup of heavy cream
- a half cup of grated Parmesan
- avocado oil (or frying oil of your choice)

INSTRUCTIONS

1. preheat oven to 400 °F
2. Green beans should be added to boiling salted water. Bring to a boil for 5 minutes. To stop cooking, drain the beans and put them in ice water. Drain and reserve.
3. Combine almond flour, coconut flour, salt, and pepper in a large mixing basin. Toss the shallots and onions until they are well coated.
4. Heat 1/2 inch of avocado oil over medium heat in a big skillet or small saucepan. Once the oil is hot, cook the breaded onions and shallots in small batches until golden and crispy.
5. Remove from oil and drain on paper towels.
6. Medium-heat a separate skillet. To the pan, add the mushrooms, butter, and garlic.
7. Approximately 8 minutes, or until the mushrooms are soft and have shed their liquid, and the garlic is fragrant.
8. Cream and stock go in the pan. Bring to a boil over medium heat, then reduce the heat to low and simmer until the mixture thickens. Once the sauce has begun to thicken, whisk in the Parmesan.

9. Add the green beans to the sauce and toss to coat them. Place the ingredients in a casserole dish. Onions and shallots are evenly distributed around the perimeter of this dish. Bake for 15 minutes.

Shredded Zucchini Casserole

Prep Time 10 mins

Cook Time 20 mins

Total Time 30 mins

Servings- 6

Ingredients

- 26 ounces grated zucchini (about 2-3 medium)
- 2 tablespoons cubed butter
- 4 ounces cubed cream cheese
- ¼ teaspoon sea salt
- pepper to taste
- 2 teaspoons shredded Parmesan cheese

Instructions

1. Grate zucchini if needed. Place in a kitchen towel and wring off excess liquid over the sink.
2. Place zucchini shreds in an 8x8-inch or 7x11-inch baking dish.
3. Spread butter evenly across zucchini.
4. Cover and bake at 350°F for 15 minutes.
5. Stir in cream cheese, salt, and pepper until the cheese has melted. Smooth top and sprinkle equally with Parmesan cheese.
6. Cover and bake for another 5 minutes.

Notes

Crushed pig rinds can replace or complement Parmesan cheese.

Loaded Creamy Cauliflower Casserole

Prep Time 15 mins

Cook Time 10 mins

Total Time 25 mins

INGREDIENTS

- 1 cauliflower head, chopped into small pieces
- split 1 cup of shredded cheddar cheese
- ½ cup mascarpone cheese
- 4 uncured bacon pieces, cooked and crumbled
- ¼ cup sour cream
- 2 teaspoons of grass-fed butter
- one tablespoon of garlic salt
- ¼ teaspoon salt
- Season with salt and pepper to taste.'
- Parsley, chopped, for garnish.'

INSTRUCTIONS

1. Preheat the oven to 450°F.
2. Place the cauliflower in a microwave-safe bowl, cover with a paper plate, and microwave for ten minutes, or until soft. Drain thoroughly and wipe gently with paper towels to dry. It must be dry so that it does not get liquid when baked.
3. Add the ingredients to a food processor's bowl. Add the other ingredients, excluding the bacon and the remaining cheddar cheese. Pulse till creamy and smooth.

4. Pour the mixture into a baking dish greased with butter and sprayed with nonstick cooking spray. Bake for 10 minutes, or until the cheese is melted and golden brown, with the remaining cheddar cheese. The dish is topped with crumbled bacon and fresh parsley.
5. Allow cooling slightly before serving.

Cheesy Low Carb Yellow Squash Casserole

Prep Time: 10 minutes

Cook Time: 45 minutes

Total Time: 55 minutes

Servings: 6 Servings

Ingredients

- 2 sliced medium Crookneck yellow squash (about 3-4 cups)
- 1 Cup Shredded Mozzarella Cheese
- 1 Cup Shredded Cheddar Cheese
- 1 1/2 teaspoons Italian seasoning
- 1 Recipe Low Carb Biscuits
- 1/2 Teaspoon Oregano
- One-half teaspoon of Onion Powder
- Half a teaspoon of Garlic Powder

Instructions

1. Preheat oven to 350 degrees.
2. Then, add the oregano, onion powder, and garlic powder to the Low Carb Biscuit dough.
3. Layer squash in a 2-quart baking dish.

4. Sprinkle with one-third of the cheese and one-third of the Italian seasonings.
5. Repeat the layering process twice more.
6. Sprinkle biscuit dough over the squash mixture.
7. Bake biscuits for 40 to 45 minutes, or until golden brown. (You must bake the biscuits for at least 40 minutes to guarantee fully baked.)

Notes

If you do not have Baking Blend, you can use almond flour, coconut flour, and flax meal in equal amounts.

Side Dishes

Keto Cranberry Sauce

YIELD 2 1/2 cups sauce
PREP TIME 2 minutes
COOK TIME 10 minutes
ADDITIONAL TIME 4 hours
TOTAL TIME 4 hours 12 minutes

Ingredients

- Twelve ounces of fresh cranberries
- 1 cup of sweetener powder, such as Lakanto
- 1 cup of water
- 1 teaspoon orange zest 5. optional 1/2 teaspoon cinnamon
- A dash of salt

Instructions

1. In a pot, boil all ingredients.
2. Simmer over medium heat, stirring intermittently, until the majority of the berries have burst. To obtain the desired texture, mash berries. As it cools, a sauce will thicken.
3. Refrigerate for four hours or until serving.

Creamy cauliflower mash with keto gravy

Total Time: 30 minutes

Yield: 8 servings 1x

INGREDIENTS

For the creamy cauliflower mash:

- 1 large cauliflower head, cored and separated into florets.
- 2 cups of chicken broth
- 5 oz. of cream cheese
- black pepper and sea salt to taste
- Olive oil used as a garnish (optional)
- parsley used as a garnish (optional)

To prepare keto gravy:

- Recipe for Herbed Butter Roasted Turkey pan drippings
- 2 cups of chicken broth
- two tablespoons of xanthan gum

HOW TO MAKE CREAMY CAULIFLOWER MASH:

1. Combine the cauliflower florets and chicken stock in a stockpot or Dutch oven.
2. Cook the stock over medium-high heat until it reaches a boil. Reduce the heat to medium-low and simmer the cauliflower for 20 minutes, or until fork-tender. While the cauliflower steams, prepare the sauce.
3. When the cauliflower is tender, remove the stock from the pan and leave the cauliflower in the hot pot for a few minutes (with the heat turned off). This will help remove extra moisture from the cauliflower so that your cauliflower mash is not soupy.
4. Place the cauliflower, cream cheese, salt, and pepper in a food processor.
5. Pulse till fluffy and smooth. Salt and pepper as needed.
6. Garnish with an olive oil drizzle and parsley, if desired.

FOR THE KETO GRAVY:
1. Remove the fat from the pan juices, reserving a small amount for flavor. Pour the residual pan juices into a saucepan from the Herbed Butter Roasted Turkey dish.
2. Combine the chicken stock and xanthan gum in a separate bowl by whisking them together.
3. Bring the gravy to a boil over medium heat after adding the stock mixture to the saucepan. Reduce the heat to low and simmer until the sauce thickens.
4. Serve the gravy with Creamy Cauliflower Mash, Herbed Butter, Roasted Turkey, and your other favorite low-carb holiday recipes.

NOTES

Gravy can be refrigerated for up to one week in a sealed jar in the refrigerator.

Cauliflower can be refrigerated for up to 5 days in an airtight container.

Low-Carb Zucchini Fries with Spicy Avocado Dipping Sauce

Prep Time10 minutes

Cook Time15 minutes

Total Time25 minutes

Servings3

Ingredients

For the zucchini fries:

- 2 zucchinis, large or 3 little zucchinis
- 1/2 cup grated coconut
- 1/2 cup almond meal
- 1 teaspoon of garlic powder
- 1 tsp smoked paprika optional
- 1 tsp cumin powder
- ¾ tsp salt
- 2 eggs

For the sauce:

- 1 avocado, medium
- 2 tablespoons plain whole-milk yogurt
- 1 tbsp lime juice
- 1 clove of crushed garlic
- 1 tsp sugar-free sriracha sauce or other hot sauce
- ¼ tsp salt
- Water to dilute

Instructions

1. Preheat oven to 450 °F (230c). Parchment lines two baking sheets.
2. The zucchinis should be halved lengthwise and then crosswise. Then, slice them into thin wedges.
3. Blend the shredded coconut in a food processor or high-powered blender until it resembles fine sand.
4. Combine the coconut, almond flour, garlic powder, smoked paprika (if using), cumin, and salt in a small bowl.
5. Separately, whisk the eggs in a small basin.
6. Each zucchini wedge is dipped in the egg, followed by the almond/coconut mixture. Ensure that both sides of the zucchini are coated.
7. Arrange the zucchini wedges on baking pans and repeat with the remaining zucchini wedges.
8. bake for 15 minutes, or until the bottom is golden brown.
9. Add all ingredients to a food processor or blender and pulse until smooth to make the sauce. Too thick? Add a tablespoon of water.
10. Serve zucchini fries immediately with dipping sauce.

Creamy Garlic Parmesan Mushroom Chicken

Prep Time: 15 minutes
Cook Time: 15 minutes
Total Time: 30 minutes
Servings: 4 people

Ingredients

For the Chicken

- 1 pound of boneless, skinless chicken breasts, or around two to three medium-sized chicken breasts
- 1 teaspoon minced garlic
- 1 teaspoon of oregano or Italian spice
- pepper and salt to taste
- 2 tbsp unsalted butter
- 1 tablespoon olive oil
- 8-ounce infant Bella mushrooms
- 1/4 cup minced onion
- 3 to 4 minced garlic cloves
- 1.5 quarts thick cream (or light cream, or half & half)
- 1 tablespoon of freshly grated parmesan cheese
- Optional: 2 teaspoons fresh herb of choice

Instructions

1. To make chicken breasts thinner, cut them in half horizontally. The chicken breasts are seasoned on both sides with garlic powder, oregano, and a sprinkle of salt and pepper.
2. Melt butter and oil in a large skillet over medium heat. Cook the chicken breasts for 5 to 6 minutes per side. Put aside the chicken.
3. In the same pan, sauté the mushrooms and onion for two to three minutes, or until soft. Add garlic, a bit of salt and pepper, and sauté for one minute or until fragrant.
4. Lower the temperature and add heavy cream, Parmesan cheese, and herbs to the dish. Simmer for 1 to 2 minutes, or until the sauce thickens. If necessary, add more salt after tasting.

5. Cook the chicken and liquids for 1-2 minutes. Serve with rice, spaghetti, salad, or vegetables.

Low Carb Cranberry Relish (keto)

Prep Time: 15 minutes

Total Time: 15 minutes

Servings: 12

Ingredients

- 12 ounces of fresh, washed Ocean Spray cranberries
- 1 medium orange 4 ounces
- 2/3 cup low carb powdered sugar or Swerve Granulated
- 1 teaspoon of fresh ginger juice (1-inch piece of fresh ginger chopped, squeeze in a garlic press)
- three pinches of clove powder

Instructions

1. Rinse the cranberries and discard any soft or small berries or stones. Cut the orange's stem and blossom end to the flesh, then quarter and halve each quarter. Avoid peeling the orange. Throw away any seeds. Chop a 1-inch piece of ginger roughly. The sweetener was ground in a coffee or spice grinder.
2. Layer the cranberries and orange segments in a food processor, then add the sweetener, spices, and ginger juice. Put the ginger into a garlic press and squeeze to obtain as much juice as possible. It cannot be tasted, yet it contributes to the overall flavor.)

3. Using the pulse button, pulse the food processor until the cranberries and orange are roughly chopped to the same size. Taste. If you want it sweeter, add your favorite stevia sweetener or additional powdered Sukrin 1 (or Swerve Granulated). It should have both sour and sweet flavors.
4. Refrigerate up to two days before use and for five to seven days. It makes roughly 3 cups, with each serving being 1/4 cup.

CRANBERRY SAUCE

Prep Time: 30 minutes
Cook Time: 4 hours 30 minutes
Total Time: 5 hours
Yield: 6 1x

INGREDIENTS

- 12 ounces of fresh cranberries
- Zest medium orange
- 1 tsp stevia
- 1/2 tsp vanilla extract
- 3/4 cup water

INSTRUCTIONS

1. In a pot, boil all ingredients.
2. Reduce the heat and simmer for fifteen minutes
3. Refrigerate for 4 hours.
4. Serve ice cold

DELICIOUSLY PERFECT KETO CREAMED SPINACH

Prep Time: 10 minutes

Cook Time: 10 minutes

Total Time: 20 minutes

Yield: 4 servings 1x

INGREDIENTS

- 4 tablespoons divided butter
- 2 tablespoons minced garlic
- Two 10-ounce bags of thawed drained frozen spinach
- Four ounces of cream cheese, cut into one-inch chunks
- 1/2 cup parmesan cheese grated
- 1/2 cup whipped heavy cream
- 1/2 tsp salt
- 1/4 tsp pepper

INSTRUCTIONS

1. In a saucepan over medium heat, sauté 3 tablespoons of butter and minced garlic for two minutes, or until aromatic. Cook spinach 5 minutes.
2. Melt the remaining 1 tablespoon of butter, cream cheese, parmesan cheese, heavy whipping cream, salt, and pepper in a small saucepan.
3. Pour cream sauce over spinach, then combine.
4. Serve without delay

CREAMY CAULIFLOWER MASHED 'POTATOES'

Prep Time: 10 minutes

Total Time: 25 minutes

INGREDIENTS

- 1 cauliflower head
- 2 tablespoons grass-fed butter
- 1 tbsp parmesan cheese
- 1/2 cup almond milk

INSTRUCTIONS

1. Heat water in a pot.
2. Place broken cauliflower chunks in boiling water and bring them to a boil.
3. Once boiling, reduce heat to a simmer for 12 to 15 minutes, or until cauliflower is tender.
4. Drain the cauliflower.
5. Use a masher to achieve the ideal texture for the cauliflower.
6. Combine milk, butter, and cheese in a blender.
7. You can serve it as is, or you can proceed to the next steps:
8. Set oven to broil.
9. Place cauliflower mash in a baking dish or skillet, then top with parmesan.
10. Broil on high until the parmesan begins to brown and get crunchy.

CRISPY KETO BACON WRAPPED ASPARAGUS

Prep Time: 5 minutes

Cook Time: 20 minutes

Total Time: 25 minutes

Yield: 12 bundles 1x

INGREDIENTS

- 36 spears of asparagus
- 12 slices of bacon
- 1 tablespoon olive oil
- Salt and black pepper to taste

INSTRUCTIONS

1. Line a baking sheet with parchment paper and preheat oven to 425°F.
2. Wrap three asparagus spears with a single slice of bacon in a spiral fashion. Place on the baking sheet that has been prepared. Continue with the remaining ingredients.
3. Drizzle with olive oil and season to taste with salt and pepper. Bake bacon until crisp, 20 to 25 minutes.

SHEET PAN BRUSSELS SPROUTS WITH BACON

Prep Time: 10 minutes

Cook Time: 35 minutes

Total Time: 45 minutes

Yield: 6 servings 1x

INGREDIENTS

- 16 ounces bacon
- 16 ounces of uncooked brussels sprouts
- Salt

- Pepper

INSTRUCTIONS

1. Preheat oven to 400 degrees Celsius. Bake with parchment paper.
2. Halve brussels sprouts.
3. Using kitchen shears, cut bacon into thin strips along its length.
4. Add brussels sprouts and bacon to the baking sheet, then season with salt and pepper.
5. Bake for 35 to 40 minutes, or until the brussels sprouts are gently browned, and the bacon is crisp.

LOW-CARB CAULIFLOWER MAC AND CHEESE

Total Time: 30 minutes

Yield: 3 cups 1x

INGREDIENTS

- 8 ounces of thick cream
- 4 ounces sharp cheddar (shredded)
- 4-ounce fontina (shredded)
- 2 ounces of cream cheese
- 1 teaspoon salt
- 1/2 teaspoon of black pepper
- 1 1/4 teaspoon paprika
- 1 huge cauliflower head

INSTRUCTIONS

1. Preheat oven to 375 °F and butter or spray an 8x8 baking dish with nonstick spray.
2. Cut cauliflower into 1/2-inch to 1-inch chunks. For 4 to 5 minutes, steam the vegetables until barely soft. Remove from heat and thoroughly drain. Use paper towels to absorb excess moisture Set aside.
3. In a small pot, combine heavy cream, cheeses, cream cheese, salt, pepper, and paprika. Melt under a moderate flame until smooth. Stir thoroughly.
4. Toss cauliflower with the cheese mixture to coat.
5. Pour into a baking dish and bake for 25 to 30 minutes, or until the top is golden and bubbling.

Drinks

KETO PUMPKIN SPICE LATTE

PREP TIME: 10 MINS

COOK TIME: 5 MINS

TOTAL TIME: 15 MINS

YIELD: 1 coffee

SERVING SIZE: 1 pumpkin spice latte

INGREDIENTS

- 2 teaspoons Pumpkin Puree (not pumpkin pie filling)
- 1/2 teaspoon Pumpkin Pie Spices
- Adjust the amount of Erythritol based on how sweet you prefer your coffee.

- ½ teaspoon Vanilla Extract
- 1 cup Sugar-Free Almond Milk
- one-half cup of robust coffee

OPTIONAL ADD-ONS FOR A BULLETPROOF PUMPKIN LATTE

- 1 teaspoon MCT Oil or, if dairy-free, coconut oil
- 1 teaspoon unsalted butter or dairy-free ghee or cocoa butter

TO PROVIDE

- 1 tablespoon Sugar-Free Vanilla Syrup
- 2 teaspoons of Unsweetened Whipping Cream
- 1 pinch of Spices for Pumpkin Pie

INSTRUCTIONS

PREPARE THE PUMPKIN SPICE MILK

1. Stir together pumpkin puree, pumpkin spices, vanilla, and erythritol over low to medium heat in a small saucepan. Stir and heat for 1 minute or until aromatic (like pumpkin pie!).
2. Stir in the unsweetened almond milk and cook the pumpkin spiced milk for one minute or until bubbles develop along the pan's edge. You can add pumpkin milk, butter, and MCT oil to a blender and blend until frothy Bulletproof pumpkin spice latte. To make a traditional keto pumpkin latte, skip this step and proceed to "build the drink."

ASSEMBLE THE LATTE

1. Pour coffee into a mug (minimum two 17fl oz cups).
2. Pour the pumpkin spiced hot milk over your coffee.
3. Serve with two tablespoons of unsweetened whipped cream, sugar-free vanilla syrup, and a dash of ground nutmeg or pumpkin spice.

4. Pumpkin pie spices: 1/4 teaspoon powdered cinnamon, 1/8 teaspoon powdered nutmeg, and 1/8 teaspoon powdered ginger

Keto Nutella Frappuccino

Total Time: 5 minutes

Servings: 1

Ingredients

- 1/2 cup unsweetened vanilla almond milk
- 1/4 cup thick heavy cream
- 1 tsp coffee granules instant
- 2 tablespoons of Swerve Confectioners
- 2 tbsp ChocZero Hazelnut Spread
- 1/4 teaspoon of xanthan gum
- 1 cup ice
- Optional keto-friendly whipped cream and hazelnut butter spread

Instructions

1. All components, excluding ice, are blended in a blender.
2. Add ice and continue blending until the ice is completely absorbed.
3. Pour the wine into a glass and enjoy!
4. Optionally, garnish with keto-friendly whipped topping.

Bulletproof Hot Chocolate

Prep Time: 5 minutes

Total Time: 5 minutes

Servings: 1

Ingredients

- one-half cup hot water (not scolding hot) (I heat mine on the stove in a small pot)
- one-half cup of unsweetened almond milk
- 2 teaspoons of coconut oil or MCT oil
- 2 tablespoons chocolate powder, unsweetened
- ¼ teaspoon vanilla
- 1-2 tablespoons of Erythritol.
- Optional heavy whipping cream

Instructions

1. In a blender, combine all of the ingredients until smooth.
2. If desired, top with Heavy Whipping Cream.

Notes

IMPORTANT: Be extremely cautious while opening a high-speed blender containing a hot liquid, as a vacuum may be created. Ensure that water is not scalding. Blend it for only a few seconds at a time, allowing the pressure to release between each blending.

I've tried this recipe using both MCT oil (which has no flavor) and coconut oil, and I preferred the MCT oil, but that's because I dislike coconut!

CHRISTMAS

Desserts

Keto Chocolate Chip Cookies

Prep Time: 10 minutes

Cook Time: 12 minutes

Total Time: 22 minutes

Servings: 21

INGREDIENTS

- 3/4 cup of melted butter or coconut oil
- ⅔ cup Granular Sweetener
- 2 Eggs
- 2 tsp Vanilla Extract
- three cups of almond meal
- ½ tsp Baking soda
- ½ tsp Kosher salt
- One-half nine-ounce Bag of Sugar-free Chocolate Chips

EQUIPMENT

- Cookie Scoop

INSTRUCTIONS

1. preheat oven 350 degrees F. 2. In a stand mixer (or big bowl with a hand mixer), combine softened butter (or coconut oil) and swerve sweetener on medium speed until incorporated.

3. add 2 eggs and vanilla and stir till blended

4. In a larger basin, combine almond flour, baking soda, and salt.

5. Blend dry and wet components.

6. Incorporate Lily's Chocolate Chips

7. Place 18 to 21 cookies on a prepared baking sheet (you may need 2 depending on how big your sheets are). Flatten them by lightly pressing down on the top.

8. Bake for 10-12 minutes

9. Allow cooling for thirty minutes on the cookie sheets. These will remain soft and tasty for at least four days when stored in an airtight container. For freezing instructions, see the notes.

JENNIFER'S TIPS

Almond Flour Free Version: So many individuals are intolerant to almonds. Substitute sunflower seed flour for almond flour. It is priced similarly to almond flour.

No Chocolate Chips from Lily's?: If you cannot get sugar-free chocolate chips, you can use a bar of dark chocolate containing 85 percent cocoa and chop it into chunks. You may need Mixing - This recipe has evolved into a dump recipe, as the cookies turn out perfectly even if all the ingredients are dumped into a large bowl and mixed.

Cookie Scoop - Guarantees evenly distributed keto chocolate chip cookies. Whenever I use my cookie scoop, I end up with 21 cookies. I provided a link to the one I use in the recipe.

I am checking for Doneness - The bottoms and tops of these keto cookies brown as they bake. My potatoes have always been cooked to perfection after 12 minutes.

I've kept these frozen for months, and they're still delicious. I freeze them on a sheet tray for two hours before transferring them to a freezer-safe container or bag. I remove one from the freezer anytime I'm in the mood for a cookie since they are so delicious right from the freezer.

LOW CARB KETO PUMPKIN CHEESECAKE RECIPE

PREP: 15 minutes

COOK: 55 minutes

TOTAL: 1 hour 10 minutes

SERVINGS: (adjust to scale recipe)

INGREDIENTS

ALMOND FLOUR CHEESECAKE CRUST

- 1 1/2 cup of Wholesome Yum Blanched Almond Flour
- 1/2 cup Vital Proteins Collagen Peptides (or whey protein powder)
- 3 tbsp Best Allulose
- One-third of a cup of unsalted butter (melted)
- 1 tsp Vanilla extract

PUMPKIN CAKE FILLING WITH CHEESE

- 24 ounces of Cream cheese (softened)
- 1 cup pumpkin puree
- 1 1/4 cup Besti Allulose Powder
- 3 big eggs (at room temperature)
- 1 tsp Pumpkin pie spice
- One-half tsp Cinnamon
- 1 tsp Vanilla extract

INSTRUCTIONS

1. Preheat oven to 350 degrees F (177 degrees C). Line the bottom of a springform pan measuring 9 inches (23 cm) with parchment paper. (You can also attempt well-greasing.)

2. To make the crust for the almond flour cheesecake, combine the almond flour, collagen or protein powder, and sugar.
3. Whisk together the melted butter and vanilla extract, then stir the mixture into the dry ingredients using a spoon or spatula until thoroughly combined. The dough will have a crumbly texture.
4. Press the dough into the prepared pan's bottom. Puncture with a fork all over. Bake for until brown. Let cool for at least 10 minutes.
5. whip the cream cheese and powdered sugar until frothy on a low to medium speed. Incorporate the pumpkin puree, pumpkin pie spice, cinnamon, and vanilla with a mixer. Beat each egg separately. (Maintain the speed of the mixer between low and medium throughout; too high a speed will introduce too many air bubbles, which is undesirable.)
6. Fill the pan's crust. The top is smoothed with a spatula. (Use a pastry spatula if you have one that fits the pan for a smoother top.)
7. Bake for 40 to 50 minutes, or until the middle is nearly set but still somewhat liquid.
8. Take the cheesecake out of the oven. If the edges are stuck to the pan, scrape them with a knife. (However, do not yet remove the springform edge.) Cool the cheesecake to room temperature on the counter, then refrigerate for at least four hours (ideally overnight) until thoroughly set. (Do not attempt to remove the cake before chilling.)
9. Serve with whipped cream or cinnamon powder.

Dark Chocolate Raspberry Cheesecake Brownies

Prep Time: 10 minutes
Cook Time: 35 minutes

Total Time: 45 minutes

Servings: 16 brownies

Ingredients

Brownie Ingredients:

- ½ cup melted butter
- one-half cup of warm water
- 2 big eggs at room temperature
- 2/3 of Joy Filled Eats Sweetener
- ½ cup almond flour
- ⅓ cup chocolate powder
- ¼ cup coconut flour
- 1 teaspoon vanilla
- ¾ teaspoon baking powder
- ¾ teaspoon salt

Topping Ingredients:

- 3.5-ounce bar of dark chocolate with 85 percent chocolate (or sugar-free chocolate of choice)
- 8 ounces of cream cheese
- divide 2 tablespoons of Joy Filled Eats Sweetener
- 1 cup of frozen raspberry

Instructions

1. Preheat oven to 350 degrees. Grease a 9-by-9-inch baking dish.
2. Whisk the butter, warm water, and eggs in a large bowl. Combine the dry ingredients thoroughly. Pour into the dish for baking. Sprinkle the chocolate crumbs over the batter.
3. Combine the cream cheese and 1 tablespoon of sweetener in a small bowl. Drop dollops onto the surface of the batter and gently stir.

4. Scatter the frozen raspberries atop the dessert. Add spoonful of the sweetener.
5. Bake for 35 to 40 minutes, or until the entire brownie has puffed and the center is no longer jiggly.

Homemade Almond Roca

Prep Time: 5 minutes
Cook Time: 10 minutes
Total Time: 15 minutes
Servings: 12 Servings

Ingredients

- 1 cup of butter
- 1/2 cup sugar white sugar, brown sugar, or substitutes for keto
- 1 cup of your preferred chocolate chips
- 1/2 cup almonds raw Cubed approximately

Instructions

1. Cover the bottom of a small square or loaf pan with parchment paper and sprinkle 1/4 cup of the chopped almonds. Set aside.
2. In a small saucepan, mix the butter and sugar. Heat until the butter has melted and the sugar has dissolved over low heat. Once the mixture begins to bubble while being continuously stirred, insert the candy thermometer into the center of the mixture. Stir every 30 seconds until the thermometer hits 300 degrees F (hard crack). Take away from the heat.

3. Continue stirring continually to prevent the separation of the butter and sugar. Pour into the prepared pan and allow it to rest for 5 minutes.
4. After 5 minutes, sprinkle the top evenly with chocolate chips. Wait 5 minutes before uncovering the pan. After 5 minutes, discard the aluminum foil. Utilizing a rubber spatula, evenly distribute the chocolate over the toffee. After spreading, sprinkle the remaining almonds on top. Refrigerate for a minimum of two hours or overnight. Upon setting, use a sharp knife to cut into pieces.

Notes

TO SAVE: Almond Roca can be stored in an airtight jar at room temperature. At least two weeks of handmade Almond Roca can be stored at room temperature. It can also be stored in the refrigerator for up to two months.
TO FROST: Wrapped in parchment paper and stored in a ziplock bag or shallow container, pieces can be frozen for six months.

Keto Peanut Butter Balls

PREP TIME 30 mins
COOL TIME 1 hr 30 mins
TOTAL TIME 2 hrs
SERVINGS 12 truffles

INGREDIENTS

- 1 cup Peanut Butter
- ½ cup Protein Powder
- 1/3 cup Honey
- 2 tsp Vanilla Extract
- ½ cup Peanut optional

For Chocolate Enrobement

- 3-ounce Baking Chocolate without sugar
- 3 tablespoons honey or confectioners' swerve
- 1 tablespoon of Olive Oil

INSTRUCTIONS

1. First, combine all the ingredients, including peanut butter, protein powder, sugar, and vanilla. Mix these ingredients in a blender or food processor until a soft dough forms.
2. (Note: if you don't like protein powder or don't have any, try almond or coconut flour for your keto diet.)
3. Then, roll the dough into 1-inch balls and arrange them in a single layer on a baking sheet or a plate. (If you notice that the dough is too soft, add additional protein powder or flour to firm it up. Or, if the dough is particularly dense, you can add low-fat or dairy-free milk to make it tender.)
4. Freeze these balls for 20 to 30 minutes to make the mixture less sticky and firm.

Chocolate glaze

1. To produce chocolate coating, chocolate, sugar, and coconut oil must be combined. Put items in microwave-safe bowl and heat in 30-second increments until smooth and melted.
2. Take the peanut butter balls out of the freezer. Insert a toothpick into the peanut butter balls, then pour them over the melted chocolate. And then, place coated balls on parchment paper and remove toothpicks from coated balls. Once more, freeze these balls for over an hour.

3. Remove from the freezer and serve as an appetizer or dessert. So delectable and yummy!

NOTES

Use chopped peanuts in the balls or topping for the chocolate coating.

Honey and maple syrup can replace sugar.

To create these balls, scoop the dough with a small cookie scoop (or a spoon). Or, if you are making the balls by hand, ensure that your hands are clean and cool.

Keto Cheese Balls

yield: 18

prep time: 10 MINUTES

additional time: 1 HOUR

total time: 1 HOUR 10 MINUTES

Ingredients

- eight pieces of cooked, chopped bacon
- 2 softened 250 g containers of cream cheese
- 1 cup cheddar cheese, shredded
- 1 teaspoon of garlic powder
- 1 tsp paprika
- 1/2 tsp salt
- 1/2 tsp pepper
- 1/4 cup chopped chives
- 1/3 cup chopped pecans

Instructions

1. Combine cream cheese, cheddar cheese, garlic powder, paprika, salt, and pepper in a large bowl. Using a cookie scoop or your hands, shape the dough into 18 little balls. Place on a platter lined with parchment paper and refrigerate for one hour.
2. Bacon, chives, and nuts in a bowl.
3. The cheese balls are rolled in the bacon mixture. Serve at room temperature or chilled.

Keto Chocolate Cake

Prep Time 25 mins
Cook Time 25 mins
Total Time 50 mins

Ingredients

- 3/4 cup almond milk, unsweetened, at room temperature
- 1/2 tbsp apple cider vinegar
- 2 cups of incredibly fine blanched almond flour
- 1/4 cup coconut flour
- 1/2 cup unsweetened cocoa powder of superior quality (can also use cacao powder if preferred)
- Optional but highly recommended for extra richness, 1/4 teaspoon espresso powder; it can be substituted with unsweetened dark cocoa powder or cacao powder if desired.
- 2/3 cup powdered monk fruit sweetener (or your preferred confectioners' sweetener), sifted
- two tablespoons of baking powder
- 1/2 teaspoon baking soda
- 1/2 teaspoon fine sea salt
- Four big room-temperature eggs, lightly beaten

- 1/2 cup melted coconut oil
- 2 teaspoons pure vanilla extract

FOR THE BUTTERCREAM:

- 2/3 cup softened grass-fed unsalted butter OR ghee
- 2.5 to 3 cups powdered monk fruit sweetener, sifted (or your preferred confectioners' sweetener) as needed to get desired consistency and sweetness.
- 1/2 cup of high-quality unsweetened cocoa powder, sifted
- two-thirds teaspoon vanilla bean paste or two teaspoons vanilla extract
- Two to three tablespoons of unsweetened almond milk, with more as needed to get desired consistency
- 1/8 teaspoon fine sea salt

DIRECTIONS

FOR THE CAKE:

1. Preheat the oven to 350 degrees Fahrenheit. Use parchment paper to line two 8-inch or three 6-inch cake pans. Set aside.
2. Combine the almond milk with apple cider vinegar in a large measuring cup. Allow it to sit (and curdle) for 5 minutes while combining the remaining ingredients.
3. In the meantime, whisk together the almond flour, coconut flour, cocoa powder, espresso powder, sweetener, baking powder, baking soda, and salt in a separate large mixing dish.
4. Add the eggs that have been beaten, coconut oil, and vanilla extract. Pour the curdled milk into the bowl and blend thoroughly.
5. Distribute the batter evenly between the two baking pans and bake in a preheated oven for 18 to 25 minutes (turning the pans halfway through), or until a toothpick is inserted into the center of the cake comes out clean. The baking time will vary based on the oven used.

6. Allow cakes to cool completely in the pan (or for at least 30 minutes) before removing them, or they may fall apart. Remove the parchment paper liner from the pan. Cool well before applying to frost.

FOR THE BUTTERCREAM FROSTING:

1. Cream the butter (or ghee) using a paddle attachment or a hand mixer on medium speed for 3 to 5 minutes.
2. Reduce the speed of the mixer to low, then gradually add the powdered sweetener and cocoa powder. Continue to combine at a low speed. Add the vanilla, milk, and salt, then increase the speed to medium and beat for two to three minutes, or until frothy. Taste and adjust the sweetener or milk to achieve consistency and sweetness.

TO ASSEMBLE THE CAKE:

1. After the cake has cooled, place the bottom layer on a dish or stand. Spread chocolate buttercream frosting before adding another layer. Add remaining frosting to the top and sides, then decorate with fresh berries as desired.
2. Cake will keep 3-5 days in the refrigerator.

Keto Pumpkin Cream Cheese Cupcakes

yield: 24

prep time: 10 MINUTES

cook time: 30 MINUTES

total time: 40 MINUTES

Ingredients

Keto Pumpkin Cream Cheese Cupcake Batter

- 1 1/2 cups of almond flour that has been finely ground, weighed, and sprinkled
- 1 1/2 teaspoons of cinnamon powder
- 1 1/2 tablespoons of ginger powder
- 1/8 teaspoon clove powder
- 1 1/2 teaspoon baking powder
- 1/4 teaspoon sea salt
- 1/2 cup of room-temperature unsalted butter
- 4 ounces of room-temperature cream cheese with full fat
- 3/4 cup of sugar-replacement granulated, I used Lakanto
- I used Lakanto Gold, 1/4 cup for the brown sugar alternative.
- 1 teaspoon of vanilla essence
- 3 big eggs, room temperature
- 1/2 cup pureed pumpkin, unsweetened

Cream Cheese Frosting for Keto

- I used Lakanto Powdered Confectioner's Sugar Substitute for 3/4 cup confectioner's sugar.
- 1/2 teaspoon vanilla extract
- 1/4 cup of room-temperature unsalted butter
- three to four teaspoons of heavy cream
- 4 ounces of softened full-fat cream cheese

<u>Instructions</u>

1. Pumpkin Cream Cheese Cupcakes on the Ketogenic Diet
2. Preheat oven to 365 °F.
3. Using cupcake liners, line two muffin tins with a total capacity of twelve muffins.
4. Sift together the almond flour, spices, and baking powder in a medium-sized basin and leave aside.

5. Next, in a separate medium-sized bowl, whip the softened butter, cream cheese, and vanilla extract using an electric mixer. In approximately two minutes, beat until light and creamy.
6. Add the pumpkin puree to this mixture and stir until completely combined.
7. Next, add the eggs one by one, alternating with the dry ingredients and mixing well after each addition.
8. Evenly distribute the cupcake batter in the muffin tin.
9. Bake for 18 to 25 minutes, or until a toothpick inserted comes out clean.
10. Wait at least half an hour for the cupcakes to cool completely before applying the cream cheese icing.

Cream Cheese Frosting for Keto

1. Electric mixer-whipped cream cheese and butter.
2. Then, add the confectioners' sugar replacement with care.
3. Next, incorporate the heavy whipping cream by adding a few tablespoons and beating until well incorporated.
4. Before icing cupcakes, let them cool fully.

Notes

Refrigerate leftovers for up to five days. The cupcakes can be frozen for three weeks, but they cannot be decorated.

Optional: Garnish the cupcakes with caramel sauce and some chopped walnuts.

Keto Chocolate Cookies

Cook Time 11 minutes

Total Time 11 minutes

Yield 8 – 12 cookies

Ingredients

- 1 cup almond flour finely milled
- 2 tablespoon cocoa powder
- scant 1/4 tsp salt
- 1/8 tsp baking soda
- 1/4 of a cup of miniature chocolate chips or sugar-free chocolate chips
- 3 tablespoons powdered sugar or erythritol
- 2 tablespoons preferred milk
- 1 tablespoon coconut oil or extra milk
- optionally coat with powdered sugar or erythritol

Instructions

1. Preheat oven to 325 degrees Fahrenheit. Stir dry ingredients very well. Add liquid to form the dough. If you're a visual learner, feel free to watch the brief video of me creating the cookies in the section above. If the dough is too wet to roll into balls with your hands or a cookie scoop, chill it until it is stiff enough. Bake for 11 minutes on a greased or parchment-lined baking sheet. If you desire flatter cookies, use a fork or spoon to press down on them. Let cool before handling. Roll in additional powdered sugar or erythritol, if desired.

Note: If you skip or reduce the number of chocolate chips, the cookies will not be as fudgy and delicious!

Keto Chocolate Crinkle Cookies

Prep Time 10 mins

Cook Time 15 mins

Total Time 25 mins

Ingredients

- 1 cup finely ground blanched almond flour
- 1/4 cup coconut flour
- 1/2 cup cocoa powder OR cacao powder, unsweetened
- 1 teaspoon baking powder
- 1/4 tsp omits the xanthan gum; however, it helps create structure.
- 1/8 teaspoon fine sea salt
- 3/4 cups of granulated monk fruit or low-carb sweetener OR coconut sugar for paleo
- 2 big eggs, room temperature
- 1/4 cups melted refined coconut oil OR avocado oil (can sub with ghee or unsalted butter if not dairy-free)
- 1 1/2 tablespoons pure vanilla extract
- 4 teaspoons granulated monk fruit sweetener or, for paleo, coconut sugar
- 3/4 cup powdered monk fruit sweetener or powdered coconut sugar for rolling (plus more as needed) (can make your own in a Vitamix)

Instructions

2. Whisk together the almond flour, coconut flour, cocoa powder, baking powder, xanthan gum, and salt in a medium bowl.
3. In the bowl of a stand mixer or using a hand mixer on high speed, combine the melted oil and granulated sweetener for three minutes, or until light and fluffy. Beat the eggs and vanilla for one minute.

4. Slowly incorporate the dry ingredients while beating on medium-low speed. Before icing cupcakes, let them cool fully. REFRIGERATE overnight or freeze 45 minutes.
5. preheat oven 350 degrees Fahrenheit and line a large baking sheet with parchment paper.
6. Remove cookie dough from the refrigerator. Place the granulated and powdered monk fruit sweetener in two small bowls.
7. Scoop and roll the mixture into 1-inch balls. Roll in granulated sweetness, then generously in powdered monk fruit sweetener, and place on a baking sheet that has been prepared.
8. Bake for 9 to 10 minutes in a preheated oven or until almost set.
9. Allow to rest for two to three minutes, or until cookies are cool enough to handle, then roll each cookie in powdered sugar and place on a clean baking sheet until all cookies are baked.
10. When cookies are nearly cooled, they should be stored in an airtight container.

Keto Christmas Cookies

Prep Time: 5 minutes
Cook Time: 12 minutes
Total Time: 17 minutes
Servings: 12 Cookies

Ingredients

- 1 cup cashew butter that is silky and runny
- 1 big egg

- 2/3 cup of your preferred granulated sweetener, erythritol, or monk fruit sweetness
- 1 teaspoon baking soda
- 1/4 cup of sugar-free candy buttons. Use only the green and red ones

Instructions

1. In a large mixing basin, thoroughly combine all ingredients except the candy buttons. Use a rubber spatula to fold the candy in towards the end.
2. Refrigerate the covered mixing bowl for 30 minutes.
3. Preheat oven to 180°C/350°F. Prepare a parchment-lined baking sheet.
4. Remove the bowl from the refrigerator. Form twelve dough balls and arrange them 1-2 inches apart on the lined baking sheet. 10 to 12 minutes, or until the edges of the cookies begin to turn golden.
5. Cool cookies to room temperature.

Notes

You may use any smooth, drippy nut or seed butter.

Use 3 to 4 teaspoons of ground chia seeds if you prepare this without eggs. Start with three tablespoons and add one more if necessary.

You may use chocolate chips or red/green ingredients such as cranberries and pistachios.

The cookies stored in an airtight container, for up to one week. If you wish to keep them longer, you can refrigerate them.

To freeze: Place cookies in a ziplock bag and keep them for up to six months in the freezer.

Snowball Cookies

PREP TIME 15 minutes

COOK TIME 10 minutes

TOTAL TIME 25 minutes

SERVINGS 24 cookies

Ingredients

- 2 ¼ cups flour
- 3/4 cup finely chopped walnuts
- ½ teaspoon salt
- 1 cup butter unsalted, softened
- 1 teaspoon vanilla
- 1/2 cup powdered sugar, plus additional sugar for dusting

Instructions

1. Preheat oven to 400 °F. Line a sheet pan with parchment paper.
1. Mix flour, chopped walnuts, and salt in a small bowl. Set aside.
2. Cream together butter, vanilla, and powdered sugar using a mixer.
3. On low, beat in the flour mixture.
4. Form dough into 1" balls, then place on the prepared baking sheet.
5. Bake cookies for 8 to 10 minutes, or until the bottom edges are gently browned.
6. Allow the cookies to cool for a few minutes till you can handle them. Roll in powdered sugar and cool fully on a cooling rack.

Recipe Notes

- In this recipe, any chopped nuts can be substituted.

- To swiftly chop nuts, give them two pulses in a food processor. They should be very finely chopped but not powdered. A few larger bits are acceptable.

German Cinnamon Stars

yield: 7 DOZEN
prep time: 10 MINUTES
bake time: 20 MINUTES
additional time: 20 MINUTES
total time: 50 MINUTES

Ingredients

- 2 1/2 cups (285 grams) of sifted powdered sugar, divided in half
- 2 1/2 to 3 cups (250 grams) almond meal or almond flour
- 1 teaspoon of cinnamon
- 4 egg whites

Instructions

1. preheat oven to 250 °F (120 degrees Celsius).
2. In a large bowl, thoroughly combine half of the powdered sugar, the ground almonds, and the cinnamon. Set aside.
3. In a bowl, beat egg whites with a mixer until soft peaks form. Add the remaining powdered sugar and continue beating for an additional 2 or 3 minutes, or until thick and creamy.
4. Set aside 1 1/4 cups (300 ml) of the beaten eggs in an airtight container (I put them in a condiment dispenser for easy decorating).
5. Combine the almond mixture with the remaining egg white mixture until a dough forms. Cover and refrigerate for 20 minutes.

6. Place some parchment paper and powdered sugar on the counter, then place the dough on top and shape it into a ball before slightly flattening it.
7. Dust the top with additional powdered sugar and set another sheet of parchment paper on top.
8. Roll out the dough to a 1/4-inch thickness, then cut out star shapes; re-roll the dough and continue to cut out stars until the dough is used up.
9. Place on a cookie sheet lined with paper or silicone, then cover with the leftover meringue mixture. Using a condiment bottle makes decorating the tops of these cookies (and others; see NOTES) a breeze.
10. Bake for 30 minutes in a warm oven, then turn off the oven, crack the door slightly, and allow to dry for another 10 minutes or so before removing. The Zimtsterne should be placed on a cooling rack to cool entirely.
11. Check the meringue mixture before coating the cookies; if it runs off, add additional sugar until it flows easily and does not run off the cookie. However, avoid making it too thick not to set smoothly.

MAIN DISHES

Roast Duck

Prep Time:15 minutes

Cook Time:2 hours

Total Time:2 hours 15 minutes

Servings: 8 Servings

Ingredients

- 1 5 - 6 Pound Duck
- 3 Tbsp. Salt

- 1 tablespoon Chinese Five Spice Powder
- 1 tablespoon of garlic powder

Instructions

1. Rinse and pat dry the duck. Remove and save the neck and giblets. Save the animal by removing extra fat from the stomach and tail area and trimming a little of the loose neck skin. Using a fine paring knife, score duck skin without penetrating the meat.
2. Combine salt, garlic powder, and five-spice powder. Season the duck well with the spice mixture. Place duck breast-side up on a rack in a roasting pan.
3. Heat oven to 350 degrees.
4. Roast the duck for two hours, removing excess fat and flipping it every 30 minutes. The duck is cooked when the thickest portion of the leg reaches an internal temperature of 165 degrees.
5. *For exceptionally crisp skin, refrigerate the seasoned duck overnight, uncovered, then bring to room temperature before roasting.

Lemon & Thyme Keto Roasted Chicken

PREP TIME 15 mins

COOK TIME 1 hr 30 mins

TOTAL TIME 1 hr 45 mins

SERVINGS 8 servings

INGREDIENTS

- 1 entire skinned chicken weighing 5 to 6 pounds
- kosher salt
- freshly ground black pepper
- 1 medium onion quartered
- twenty spring thyme

- 2 tablespoons extra virgin olive oil
- eight to ten finely sliced garlic cloves
- four medium shallots, peeled and cut lengthwise into quarters
- 2 bunches of trimmed and halved medium radishes
- 1/4 cup optional olives
- 1 lemon crosswise sliced thinly
- two-thirds cup of dry white wine or chicken broth
- 2 tablespoons blackstrap molasses or your preferred sweetener

INSTRUCTIONS

1. Preheat the oven to 425 °F or 220 degrees Celsius.
2. Rinse and pat dry the chicken from the inside out. Whenever necessary, remove any remaining pin feathers. Salt and freshly ground black pepper liberally applied to the interior of the bird. Stuff the cavity with the onion quarters, garlic, and a portion of the thyme. Kitchen string is used to connect the legs.
3. Pour olive oil over the baking sheet. Spread the remaining garlic, shallots, radishes, and olives on the bottom of the pan. On top of the prepared chicken, arrange the remaining lemon slices and thyme sprigs.
4. Thoroughly combine white wine (or broth) and molasses (or sweetener). Pour over the cooked chicken and vegetables. Generously season the chicken's exterior with salt and freshly ground black pepper.
5. Roast for 1 1/2 hours, or until the leg and thigh juices run clear. A thermometer near the bone should register at least 165 degrees F (75 degrees Celsius). 20 minutes before serving, rest the chicken.
6. I also enjoy serving the chicken with lemon wedges that have been caramelized. After a lengthy roasting period, the vegetables acquire a delicious flavor and caramelize to perfection, becoming entirely edible. However, if you don't like them, simply remove them after roasting.

NOTES

If no shallots are available, you may use red onion.

Two good sweeteners here are Lakanto Golden and Sukrin Gold.

Please note that the estimated nutritional information includes the vegetables.

Gluten-Free & Keto Swedish Meatballs

PREP TIME 20 mins

COOK TIME 20 mins

TOTAL TIME 40 mins

SERVINGS 6

INGREDIENTS

- divide 4 tablespoons of grass-fed butter
- 1 medium white onion, chopped finely
- Five hundred grams of ground beef chuck performs admirably!
- 1/4 cup ground almonds or pork rinds (see notes!)
- 1/2 teaspoon kosher salt
- 1/4 teaspoon freshly ground black pepper
- 1/4 teaspoon cinnamon
- 1/4 teaspoon nutmeg
- 1/4 teaspoon of garlic powder
- 1 egg lightly beaten
- Divide 1/2 cup of heavy cream
- olive oil extra virgin for cooking
- one to two cups of beef broth to taste
- 1 teaspoon Dijon mustard
- 1/2 to 1 teaspoon arrowroot or konjac (glucomannan) powder or 1/4 teaspoon
- Serving suggestions

- cauliflower mashed
- Cranberry relish is an excellent substitute for lingonberry jam.

INSTRUCTIONS

1. Melt one tablespoon of butter over medium heat in a skillet or pan. Cook onion and salt until caramelized (6-8 minutes). Cool down.
2. In a bowl, combine the ground meat, almond flour (or pig rind 'panko'), salt, spices, sautéed onion, egg, and 2 tablespoons of heavy cream. Combine everything thoroughly with your hands and form them into balls (20 small-is ones or 14 large).
3. In a skillet, brown the meatballs on all sides over medium heat. You will need to rotate them several times to ensure that they cook evenly. Cover the meat with aluminum foil while you prepare the sauce.
4. Add the remaining butter to the skillet and fry until it begins to brown (do not clean the meatball remnants, as they impart flavor to the sauce!). 5. Remove the meatball remnants from the pan and set them aside. Deglaze the pan with the broth, remaining heavy cream, and mustard. Allow to simmer for a few minutes, and create a slurry with your preferred thickener (i.e., mix it with a couple of tablespoons of cold water before adding it to avoid clumping). Continue simmering until the sauce begins to thicken, then season to taste.
5. Return the meatballs to the skillet, simmer for a few more minutes, and serve immediately (maybe over mashed cauliflower!).

SIDE DISHES AND SAUCES

Keto Stuffing

Prep Time: 10 minutes

Cook Time: 40 minutes

Total Time: 50 minutes

Servings: 6

Equipment

- Baking Sheet
- 12-inch Skillet
- Measuring Cups
- Measuring Spoons

Ingredients

- 1 pound of hot or mild sausage in bulk
- less than ten ounces For mirepoix, use 1 10-ounce bag or 1/2 cup sliced onions, carrots, and celery.
- 1 4-ounce Bag of Keto Croutons
- 1 teaspoon Kosher salt
- 1 teaspoon pepper
- 2 to 3 tablespoons of chicken seasoning
- one cup of Chicken Stock
- 1 Egg, beaten

Instructions

1. Preheat the oven to 350°F. Spray a baking pan and set it aside.
2. In a 12-inch skillet, brown the sausage, add the mirepoix and simmer for two minutes.
3. Pour stock, salt, pepper, and poultry spice into the pan.
4. Add croutons and toss them in. Cover the hot pan. Allow the croutons to absorb most of the water and soften.

5. In the interim, beat the egg. After the croutons have softened, combine the egg with them.
6. Stuff the baking dish.
7. Bake for 20 to 30 minutes, or until the stuffing is firm and the top is golden brown.
8. If you prefer to use a different type of low-carb bread (such as Sola bread, Boxed Kitchen Bread, or L'oven Fresh), I recommend toasting it beforehand to ensure crispy.
9. You may use this to fill a turkey just like you would with any other stuffing recipe.

Keto Roasted Potatoes

PREP TIME 10 mins
COOK TIME 50 mins
TOTAL TIME 1 hr
SERVINGS 4 side-dish servings

INGREDIENTS

- 7 ounces of small to medium radishes, peeled and halved or sliced* 2. 2 tablespoons of extra virgin olive oil or to taste
- 2 tablespoons fresh or dried thyme (optional)
- flaky sea salt to taste
- black pepper that has been freshly ground to taste
- 1/4 cup freshly grated Parmesan cheese

INSTRUCTIONS

1. Heat oven to 400F/200C. Brush olive oil into a baking dish or rimmed tray.
2. Add radishes to the prepared baking dish, drizzle with olive oil, sprinkle with thyme (optional), and pepper and salt to taste. Roast for 45 to 60 minutes, flipping them halfway through, until brown and crisp.
3. Sprinkle Parmesan cheese on top and continue roasting for another 5 minutes. Serve immediately.
4. NOTES Daikon radishes are also effective! Simply slice them thinly and ensure evenly covered with olive oil.
5. provided is estimated for a 50g portion of raw radishes (about 10 medium radishes).

Cauliflower Mash - Keto Friendly

Prep Time: 10 mins
Cook Time: 10 mins
Total Time: 23 mins
Servings: 5 serves

Ingredients
- 1 medium Cauliflower, roughly 1.4 pounds
- 3 ounces of Butter
- 1 teaspoon salt
- 1/2 teaspoon Pepper

Directions
1. Heat a lot of water.
2. Cut the cauliflower into florets of uniform size.

3. Add the cauliflower to the boiling water with care and cook for 5-8 minutes, or until soft.
4. Thoroughly drain the cauliflower and return it to the warm pot.
5. Add butter, salt, and pepper to the dish.
6. Blend the cauliflower until there are no lumps with a stick blender.
7. Allow the mash to rest for three minutes before blending it again. This stage of resting and blending the cauliflower makes it extremely smooth and creamy.
8. Serve with pleasure.

KETO CHEESY ASPARAGUS RECIPE

PREP: 5 minutes

COOK: 15 minutes

TOTAL: 20 minutes

INGREDIENTS

- 1 pound Asparagus (trimmed)
- 2 tablespoons Olive oil
- 2 teaspoons Italian seasoning (divided)
- Sea salt
- Black pepper
- 1/2 cup Mozzarella cheese (shredded)
- 1/2 cup grated Parmesan (shredded)

INSTRUCTIONS

- Preheat oven to 400 degrees Fahrenheit (204 degrees C). Line a baking sheet with greased aluminum foil or parchment paper.

- Combine olive oil, sea salt, black pepper, and a teaspoon of Italian spice with the asparagus. Arrange the ingredients in a single layer on the baking sheet.
- Roast in the oven for around 7 to 9 minutes, or until the asparagus is brilliant green and soften.
- Mix the mozzarella and Parmesan cheeses, then sprinkle over the asparagus. Add the remaining teaspoon of Italian spice on top.
- Return to oven for 6 to 8 minutes until the cheese has melted and turned golden brown.

Keto Cranberry Sauce Recipe (Sugar-Free)

Cook Time 10 mins

Total Time 10 mins

Servings 6

INGREDIENTS

- 300 g / 10.5 oz frozen cranberries
- 90 g / 3/4 cup erythritol powder
- 1 tablespoon brandy is optional
- 100 ml / 3.5 oz water scant ½ cup

INSTRUCTIONS

1. Put all the ingredients into a saucepan. Bring water to a boil.
2. Reduce heat to medium and simmer for approximately 10 minutes, stirring periodically.

SNACKS AND NIBBLES

Keto Almond Flour Crackers

Prep Time 20 mins
Cook Time 15 mins
Rest time 15 mins
Total Time 50 mins
Servings: 6 servings

INGREDIENTS

- 2 cups blanched almond flour that has been finely milled 2 cups of Bob's Red Mill Super-Fine Almond Flour is equivalent to 8 ounces. It is preferable to measure by weight rather than by volume.
- ▫1 big egg
- one teaspoon of Diamond Crystal kosher salt or half a teaspoon of sea salt
- "Your selection of toppings" I utilize Everything except the Bagel seasoning, crushed red pepper, and coarse salt.

INSTRUCTIONS

1. Preheat the oven to 350 °F. Wrap a baking sheet in parchment paper.
2. Combine the almond flour, egg, and kosher salt in a larger bowl. Mix with a rubber spatula and then your hands until a dough forms. If necessary, add 1-2 teaspoons of water.
3. Hand-transfer dough to parchment-lined baking sheet. It was pressed into a disc. Cover with another sheet of parchment and roll out as thinly as possible (approximately 1/8 of an inch).
4. Using a pizza cutter, cut the dough into 1-inch squares after removing the top layer of parchment paper.
5. Gently separate the squares so that none of them are touching.

6. Reroll the pieces between two additional sheets of parchment. Cut additional crackers and place them on the baking sheet. Place the dough in the freezer for a few minutes if it gets too soft and difficult to manipulate.
7. Sprinkle the toppings over the crackers. Place another layer of paper over the crackers and roll them gently to help the toppings cling.
8. Bake for 15-20 minutes, or until the crackers are golden brown and crunchy. If you, like me, we're unable to spread out your dough uniformly, you will need to remove the thinner crackers first, then return the remaining crackers to the oven for additional baking.
9. Before consuming the crackers, allow them to cool for at least 15 minutes, preferably 30 minutes, on a wire rack.
10. Once totally cooled, place the leftovers in an airtight jar on the counter for up to three days or the refrigerator for one week. Before serving, reheat the chips in a 350°F oven for 5 minutes if they have been refrigerated.

KETO SALT AND VINEGAR CHIPS

PREP TIME: 10 mins
COOK TIME: 12 hrs
TOTAL TIME: 20 hrs 10 mins
SERVINGS: 6

Ingredients

SALT AND VINEGAR SEASONING

- 90 g salt flakes

- 45 grams of white vinegar
- 1/2 teaspoon xanthan gum

CHIPS

- 1 large cucumber from the continent, finely sliced into rounds
- 2 large zucchinis, thinly sliced into rounds
- sixty grams of white vinegar or apple cider vinegar

<u>Instructions</u>

1. Combine all seasoning ingredients in a small bowl. Allow to dry overnight on a sheet of baking paper or use a dehydrator. (If the seasoning is still moist on the baking paper, simply pull it off and flip it over.)

Place the cucumber and zucchini in a basin that is not reactive. Pour the vinegar into the bowl and stir to coat the ingredients. Place in the refrigerator overnight to marinate.

3. Grind the seasoning with a mortar and pestle or pulse for 10 seconds at speed 5 in a blender/Thermomix® to create a fine seasoning.

4. Arrange the chips in a single layer on dehydrator trays or baking sheets, then liberally sprinkle with spice. Dry at 55 to 60 degrees Celsius for 8 to 12 hours until crisp. (this will depend on the thickness of your chip) Alternately, dehydrate until dry and crisp in the oven at 60°C.

Notes

INGREDIENTS

Xanthan gum - xanthan gum is utilized to absorb the vinegar. While the salt absorbs the vinegar, the xanthan gum forms a paste that dries quickly and maybe pulverized into a powder that adheres to the chips. I do not suggest omitting it. Xanthan gum does not cause gummy chips or a weird mouthfeel.

This meal can be made with any low-carb vegetables. You may also substitute chokos (chayote), squash, turnips, swedes, sweet potato, and pumpkin for the vegetables listed above.

I use a dehydrator to produce these chips, but a low oven set to 60°C can also work. If the oven is static, it may take longer for the chips to become thoroughly dry and crisp. Simply continue frying until crisp.

STORAGE

Chips may be stored in an airtight, dry container for 30 days. If the chips get mushy over time, they can be re-dehydrated to restore their crispness.

No-Bake Whole30 Energy Balls

Prep Time: 1 minute

Cook Time: 4 minutes

Total Time: 5 minutes

Servings: 18 Balls

Ingredients

- For the whole 30 and paleo version
- 1/4 cup cashews raw
- 3/4 cup uncooked almonds
- 1 1/2 cups Medjool dates
- 1/4 cup cocoa powder
- For the keto alternative
- 1 Chocolate Keto Energy Balls

Instructions

1. Blend or process the nuts in a high-powered blender or food processor until a crumbly texture remains. Over-blending will result in the formation of nut butter.
2. Add your Medjool dates and blend until the mixture is thick and uniform. Add chocolate powder. Continue blending or pulsing, scraping the edges frequently to ensure complete mixing.
3. In a large bowl, pour the chocolate energy ball batter. The dough should be formed into little balls, placed on a plate lined with plastic wrap, and refrigerated for 10 minutes or until firm.

Keto Trail Mix

Prep Time: 1 minute

Cook Time: 0 minutes

Total Time: 1 minute

Servings: 12 servings

Ingredients

- 1/2 cup sugar-free sugar-coated pecans
- 1/2 cup sugar-free almond confections
- 1/2 cup keto milk, white and dark chocolate chips
- 1 cup sugar-free nut confections
- a half-cup of coconut cashews

Instructions

1. In a mixing bowl, combine all the ingredients and stir until well mixed.
2. Pour into separate baggies or jars and shut to prevent more moisture from forming.

Notes

This trail mix can be personalized. Use any desired nuts or seeds.

STORAGE: Store leftover trail mix in an airtight container at room temperature for two months.

The trail mix can be frozen in a ziplock bag for six months.

Keto Granola Bars

Prep Time: 5 minutes
Cook Time: 20 minutes
Total Time: 25 minutes
Servings: 12 servings

Ingredients

- 1 cup uncooked almonds
- 1/2 cup chopped raw cashew nuts
- 2 tbsp optional pumpkin seeds
- half a cup of keto crisp cereal
- 5 tbsp keto maple syrup

Instructions

1. Preheat oven to 180°C/350°F. Line an 8 × 8-inch baking dish with parchment paper and generously oil it. Set aside.
2. Combine your nuts and seeds with your cereal in a large mixing dish. Pour the sugar-free syrup over the nuts/cereal and thoroughly blend until everything is evenly coated with the syrup.
3. Transfer the granola bar mixture to the prepared pan and push it down evenly with a rubber spatula to create a uniform layer. Bake for 25 minutes.
4. Cool the bars completely before slicing.

Notes

- Granola bars are delicate and sticky, so they must be stored in the refrigerator. Keep them covered for up to four weeks, and they will remain fresh.
- Individually wrap bars in parchment paper and place them in a Ziploc bag. Freeze bars for up to six months.

Keto Tortilla Chips

Prep Time: 5 minutes
Cook Time: 12 minutes
Servings: 8 servings

Ingredients

- 1 cup blanched almond flour almond flour
- 2 cups shredded mozzarella cheese
- 1 teaspoon of desired seasonings (pepper, paprika, etc.).

Instructions

1. Preheat oven to 180°C/350°F. Line a sheet pan with parchment paper.
2. Add almond flour to a large mixing bowl and leave aside. Melt the mozzarella cheese for one to two minutes in a microwave-safe bowl.
3. Transfer the melted cheese to the bowl of almond flour and thoroughly combine until a thick dough is formed.
4. Put parchment on the counter. Place the dough ball on it and lightly flatten it. Place the second parchment paper sheet on top. Roll out the dough to 1/6-inch thickness and flatness.
5. Cut pizza dough into triangles. Place the uncooked tortilla chip pieces on the prepared baking sheet.
6. Bake the tortilla chips for 12 to 15 minutes, or until golden brown. Remove from the oven and allow to cool completely on the baking sheet.

Notes

1. Avoid using other types of shredded cheese or even mozzarella with reduced-fat.
2. Store keto tortilla chips in an airtight jar at room temperature.

Keto Cheese Chips

Prep Time: 1 minute

Cook Time: 8 minutes

Total Time: 9 minutes

Servings: 4 servings

Ingredients

- 1 cup of grated cheese. I used cheddar
- 1 tbsp optional Parmesan cheese

Instructions

1. Preheat oven 200°C/400°F. Large baking sheet lined with parchment paper and generously greased. Set aside.

Place heaping tablespoons of shredded cheese on the baking sheet that has been buttered. The tops are sprinkled with parmesan cheese.

3. Bake for seven to ten minutes, or until golden brown. Remove from the oven and allow to cool on the baking sheet for 10 minutes before moving to a cooling rack.

Notes

It is ideal to use Cheddar cheese, however, mozzarella and pepper jack may also be used. Do not use cheese slices.

Cheese crisps can be stored for one week in a completely sealed container. Any longer and its crispiness will begin to diminish.

To freeze: Place leftovers in a vacuum-sealed or sturdy Ziploc bag and freeze for up to six months.

BREAD AND LOAFS

Keto Pull-Apart Bread for Christmas

yield: MAKES 24 "BREAD" ROLLS

prep time: 20 MINUTES

cook time: 15 MINUTES

total time: 35 MINUTES

Ingredients

- 3 cups shredded mozzarella
- 4 tablespoons cream cheese
- 2 1/4 cups almond meal
- 2 eggs, beaten
- black pepper
- 5 mozzarella cheese strings, each sliced into five pieces
- ¼ cup (2 oz) butter, melted
- one-fourth cup grated Parmesan
- 2 tablespoons of cut fresh basil
- ½ tsp red pepper flakes, optional

Instructions

1. Preheat the oven to 375 degrees F.

2. To make dough, microwave mozzarella and cream cheese for one minute. Stir, then cook for a further thirty seconds Repeat until all of the mozzarellas has melted.
3. Add the almond flour, beaten egg, and pepper to the mixture. Mix thoroughly to mix. Allow the dough to cool until it is manageable, then knead until smooth. Add additional almond flour if the mixture is too sticky to handle.
4. Form a tiny ball that is then flattened. Place a string cheese piece in the center. Fold the dough around the string cheese and ensure that every seam is sealed. Place on a sheet pan coated with a silicone baking mat or parchment paper. Continue with the remaining dough, arranging the balls into a tree shape.
5. Roast for 10 to 12 minutes, or until golden. In the interim, mix Parmesan into the melted butter. Transfer it to a serving tray with care when the bread is baked, then butter each roll.
6. Garnish with thinly sliced fresh basil and, if desired, red pepper flakes, and serve warm.

Keto Gingerbread Loaf

Prep 10 mins
Cook 1 hr
Total 1 hr 10 mins
Yield 9 servings

Ingredients

- 4 big eggs
- 1/2 cup sour cream
- 1/4 cup unsalted butter melted
- 1 cup brown sugar from Swerve
- 1 tablespoon ginger powder
- 1 tablespoon of pumpkin spice
- 1/2 tsp salt
- 2 cups almond flour, blanched
- 2 tsp baking powder
- Optional toppings include Swerve confectioners' sweetener or Keto Cream Cheese Frosting.

Instructions

1. Preheat oven to 325 °F. Line a loaf pan measuring 9 by 5 inches with parchment paper.
2. Combine the eggs, sour cream, melted butter, Swerve, ginger, pumpkin pie spice, and salt in a medium bowl.
3. Smoothly incorporate the almond flour and baking powder.
4. Transfer the batter to the prepared baking dish. Bake for 50-60 minutes. a toothpick into the center of the gingerbread and it comes out clean, the gingerbread is done.
5. Allow the gingerbread to cool on a wire rack before slicing it into 1-inch thick pieces. Serve with keto cream cheese frosting or confectioner's Swerve dusted on top.

Quick Cream Cheese Keto Pumpkin Bread

Prep Time: 15 minutes

Cook Time: 50 minutes

Total Time: 1 hour, 5 minutes

Yield: 16 1x

Ingredients

For the cream filling:

- 8 ounces cheese spread
- 1/4 cup Stevia or another granulated low-carb sweetener
- 1 tbsp coconut flour
- 1 egg
- 1 tsp orange zest
- To prepare the pumpkin bread:
- 2 cups of almond flour
- 2 tsp baking powder
- 2 tsp pumpkin pie spice
- 1/2 tsp cinnamon
- ¼ tsp nutmeg
- 3 eggs
- 1/4 cup Stevia or another granulated low-carb sweetener
- ¼ cup coconut oil, melted
- 1 cup organic pumpkin puree, canned or homemade, well-drained

Instructions

1. Preheat the oven to 350°F.

2. Line a loaf pan measuring 8 by 4 inches with parchment paper. Set aside.
3. To create the filling, combine all ingredients in a bowl and mix until uniform. Set aside.
4. Add the almond flour, baking powder, pumpkin spices, cinnamon, nutmeg, and a pinch of salt to make the bread. Set aside.
5. In the bowl of a stand mixer fitted with the paddle attachment, beat the eggs and granulated sweetener for 3 to 5 minutes, or until pale and fluffy.
6. Add the coconut oil and pumpkin puree, then beat until thoroughly blended.
7. Mix the almond flour mixture until it is smooth.
8. Pour one-half of the pumpkin batter into the loaf pan.
9. Place the cream cheese mixture on this layer, followed by the remaining pumpkin batter.
10. 50 to 60 minutes in a preheated oven, or until a toothpick inserted into the center comes out clean.
11. Cool completely before serving.

Cream Cheese Filled Keto Pumpkin Bread

Prep Time 10 mins
Cook Time 1 hr
Total Time 1 hr 10 mins
Servings 12

Ingredients

- 8 ounces of cream cheese
- 1/4 cup erythritol powder or Swerve confectioners
- one-fourth of a teaspoon of stevia extract powder
- 1 tablespoon coconut flour
- 1 egg
- 1 teaspoon citrus extract (orange or lemon)
- 1 2/3 cups almond flour
- 1 ½ teaspoon baking powder
- ½ teaspoon salt
- 1/2 teaspoon cinnamon powder
- 1/2 tsp ground cloves
- ½ teaspoon pumpkin pie spice
- 1 cup pumpkin puree
- 1/2 cup coconut oil or other oil
- 5 eggs
- 3/4 cup erythritol powder or Swerve confectioners
- 3/4 teaspoon stevia extract powder

<u>Instructions</u>

1. Preheat the oven to 325 °F (165 degrees C). Grease or spray two loaf pans lightly.

In a bowl, mix cream cheese, 1/4 cup powdered erythritol, 1/4 tsp stevia extract, 1 tsp coconut flour, 1 egg, and orange extract until smooth. Set aside. Separately, combine 1 2/3 cups almond flour, baking powder, salt, cinnamon, cloves, and pumpkin pie spice in a separate dish; leave aside.

3. Place pumpkin, vegetable oil, 5 eggs. In a large dish, combine 3/4 cup erythritol and 3/4 teaspoon stevia extract; mix thoroughly. Just until

incorporated, stir the pumpkin mixture into the flour mixture. Pour one-fourth of the pumpkin mixture into each loaf pan. Spread cream cheese mixture on top of this layer, followed by a quarter of the remaining batter.

4. 50 to 60 minutes in a preheated oven, or until a toothpick comes out clean. Transfer bread from pans to a cooling rack after 10 minutes.

Notes

- Avoid spreading the cream cheese filling too close to the edges. Otherwise, it can be apparent on the exterior of the bread.
- Alternately, chocolate chips can be incorporated into the filling or dough. The bread can also be topped with a low-carb streusel consisting of chopped nuts, cinnamon, sugar, and a small amount of low-carb flour.
- Makes 2 loaves (about 24 slices)

Drinks

Paleo & Keto Hot Chocolate With Marshmallows

PREP TIME 5 mins
COOK TIME 5 mins
TOTAL TIME 10 mins
SERVINGS 1 mug

INGREDIENTS

For the keto hot chocolate

- 1 cup almond milk
- 1 tbsp cocoa powder
- 1 to 2 tablespoons of xylitol or erythritol (to taste)

- pinch pink Himalayan salt
- 1/8 teaspoon of konjac root powder, 1/4 teaspoon of arrowroot/xanthan gum, or 1 tablespoon of chia seeds.

INSTRUCTIONS

1. Bring the milk of choice, cocoa powder, sweetener, and salt to a simmer in a small saucepan over medium heat. Adjust sweetness according to taste. Make a slurry with a tiny amount of konjac root powder and a couple of tablespoons of water; dissolve the powder well to avoid lumps. Whisk it into the hot chocolate, and simmer until the mixture thickens. Feel free to alter the quantity to your desired consistency.

Serve with (an abundance of) marshmallows.

Note: If adding arrowroot, you must also create a slurry; however, xanthan gum can be added straight (works best with an immersion blender, though). And chia seeds must be thoroughly mixed to prevent lumps.

NOTES

Please be aware that cacao and cocoa nutritional values vary; check your nutrition labels (I used Valrhona!)

Keto Hot Chocolate

Prep Time: 1 minute

Cook Time: 5 minutes

Total Time: 6 minutes

Servings: 2 servings

Ingredients

- 3 tbsp cocoa powder
- 2 tablespoons monk fruit sweetener or erythritol in place of brown sugar
- 2 cups of desired milk. I utilized almond milk that was not sweetened.
- 1/4 teaspoon vanilla extract
- 2 tsp of keto chocolate chips
- one-quarter cup keto marshmallows
- 1/4 cup of keto-friendly whipped cream

Instructions

1. Combine cocoa powder, your preferred sweetener, milk, and vanilla extract in a small saucepan. Bring the liquid to a boil over a medium heat setting. When it begins to boil, turn off the heat.
2. Add chocolate chunks and let them sit for a few minutes before mixing the mixture.
3. Pour the mixture into two mugs, then garnish with marshmallows and whipped cream.

Notes

ON STORAGE: Hot chocolate is best served fresh, but leftovers can be refrigerated and covered, for up to 5 days if you prepare a larger quantity.

To move forward: Reheat the hot chocolate in 30-second increments in the microwave or a small pot on the stove. Once hot, stir in marshmallows and/or whipped cream, then serve.

KETO MATCHA LATTE

PREP TIME: 5 MINS

TOTAL TIME: 5 MINS

YIELD: 1 latte

SERVING SIZE: 1 latte

INGREDIENTS

- 1 teaspoon Matcha Powder
- 3 teaspoons Warm Water
- two to three teaspoons of erythritol or one to two drops of liquid stevia
- ⅓ cup Heavy Cream or full-fat coconut cream
- 3/4 cup Sugar-Free Almond Milk

INSTRUCTIONS

1. Whisk Matcha powder and lukewarm water in a small pot until no lumps remain.
2. Add heavy cream, your preferred sweetener, and half a cup of almond milk; the remaining almond milk will be used in your milk frother. In the absence of a milk frother, add the entire 3/4 cup of almond milk at this point.
3. Warm till medium heat, approximately 2 to 3 minutes, or until heated.
4. Serve in a coffee mug and, if wanted, top with frothed almond milk.
5. Garnish with a pinch of additional Matcha powder; this will not add any net carbohydrates.

Keto Christmas Margarita

PREP TIME 10 mins
COOK TIME 2 mins
TOTAL TIME 12 mins

SERVINGS 2

INGREDIENTS

- 2.5 cups of Water
- 3 buddha organic cranberry tea bags
- 1 tablespoon of lime juice
- 1/4 teaspoon of orange extract
- Keto sweetener of preference for flavor
- 3 oz. of your choice of gold or silver tequila
- Garnish with fresh cranberries and lime slices
- Ice

INSTRUCTIONS

1. Place the tea bags and water in a microwave-safe bowl or container. Heat for two minutes, then steep for another five. Remove and discard the tea bags.
2. Add lime juice, orange extract, your preferred sweetener, and tequila to the tea mixture, and stir until thoroughly combined.
3. Two glasses are filled with ice.
4. Pour the cocktail mixture over ice and garnish with lime slices and fresh cranberries.

Printed in Great Britain
by Amazon